D0218931

SHEET METAL CUTTING

Collected Articles
and
Technical Papers

Edited by
A. Nickel

Published by
Fabricators & Manufacturers Association, International
Rockford, Illinois

Contents

- -

Chapter Three: Thermal Cutting

Chapter Four: Waterjet

Chapter Five: Other Technologies

Preface

- -

This textbook is a compilation of selected articles on sheet metal cutting that have appeared in The FABRICATOR® and conference proceedings books from Fabricators & Manufacturers Association, International (FMA).

These articles were originally published between January 1989 and July 1993. However, for the publication of this textbook, all authors were asked to update their material if necessary, so that even articles from four years ago will contain information relevant to today's sheet metal cutting operations.

This textbook is not intended to be a complete account of sheet metal cutting technology. It is limited to the scope of articles we have already published. However, a vast array of knowledge shared by these experts over the past four years is presented here, and the articles cover many important sheet metal cutting topics.

The publishing of an article in this textbook should not be seen as an indication of endorsement of any company, author, technique, or equipment by Fabricators & Manufacturers Association, International.

The editor would like to thank the authors for their participation and help in preparing this book. Organizational and production help from Sherry Young, Graphic Designer, is also gratefully acknowledged.

A. Nickel
Editor

Chapter 1

Sawing

Selecting a metal cutting saw:
How to avoid buying
the wrong machine

For most fabricators, a metal sawing operation is needed. Metal cutting machine tool manufacturers have responded by producing a variety of machines to meet any metal sawing application. The broad selection of machines is good news for any fabricator interested in purchasing a saw.

With a little research, the proper saw for the work to be done is readily available at the right price. Before selecting a saw, a thorough survey of the range of metal cutting technologies should be made to ensure that the machine selected performs the optimum desired cut at the minimum price.

The greatest concentration of metal sawing requirements is for machines that cut structurals and solids in the 10-inch range and smaller. For this cutting, three primary types of saws are generally used:

1. Cold saws
2. Vertical band saws
3. Horizontal band saws

Each of these saw configurations has several variations designed to respond to specific sawing requirements.

Cold Saws

The type of saw commonly referred to as cold saw, or sometimes **circular saw**, employs a circular, hardened steel blade approximately ⅛-inch thick, with deep blade gullets to remove metal. The blade travels at a very low revolutions per minute (RPM) range, typically between 15 and 90 RPM, and the deep gullets remove a long, curled chip similar to the chip produced in a milling operation.

Unlike the heat generated by the friction of high-speed band sawing, cold saws generate little heat because of the slow blade speed — hence the designation "cold" saw.

In the cold saw category, four common design types exist:

1. Vertical column (see **Figure 1-1**)
2. Pivot head
3. Trunnion advanced up-acting
4. High-speed nonferrous (see **Figure 1-2**)

A fabricator that cuts small solids, structurals, tubing, or aluminum extrusions and requires tight tolerances with a mill-like finish and little or no burr should consider cold saw metal removal technology to attain these cutting finish characteristics.

Typically, a cold saw prospect cuts high-volume quantities of the same material. Each individual piece part is required to maintain specific tolerance values, and all the cuts and tolerances must be performed on a repeatable basis.

Once a cold saw has been set up for a specific application by selecting the correct blade configuration and cutting speed, a cold saw can be more forgiving of operator error

Figure 1-1. A vertical column cold saw designed to give a burr-free, accurate cut is shown here.

than a band saw. The key element of cold saw cutting to achieve the desired result — repeatable, high-tolerance piece parts in volume — is operator training in blade applications, feed rates, and spindle speed.

A pegboard near the saw with a grid that shows the blade sizes and tooth numbers, the material to be cut, and the feed and spindle rate settings is one practical system for assuring optimum cutting performance used by many fabricators who cut a variety of materials on a regular basis. This same information can be stored in a personal computer (PC) database for operator retrieval.

By using documentation and employing a simple setup system, most cutting problems can be avoided and substantial money saved on blade resharpening. A cold saw should not be considered for an uncontrolled shop setting unless proper training is available for all potential users.

Most cold saw manufacturers provide some type of demonstration and sample material cutting program for prospective clients. This is an excellent way to determine if the cold saw metal

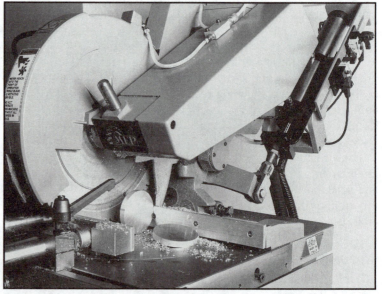

Figure 1-2. This is an example of a high-speed saw used for nonferrous applications.

cutting method is the right selection for the job. A blade recommendation is also provided by the saw manufacturer for the material to be cut.

Initially, cold saw blades seem expensive. However, they can be resharpened many times at a nominal fee. Carbide-tipped blades are available for nonferrous applications that require high RPM cold saws. Because cold saw blades are circular solid disks, a great degree of accuracy can be achieved if close tolerances are needed.

Horizontal Band Saws

Horizontal band saws use a continuous loop saw blade that revolves on two large wheels, one of which is under power. A section of the blade between the two wheels is held rigid by a pair of fixed, rigid blade guides, and the metal cutting takes place between the guides.

The workpiece is held in place by a vise. The cutting head either descends from a pivot point or down one or two wide columns. The rate of cutting descent is controlled by an hydraulic or servo-activated valve.

Like cold saws, horizontal band saws are produced in many different configurations, such as twin column, single column, and pivot head saws (see **Figure 1-3**). Some, but not all, can cut miters.

The material being cut can be fed, clamped, and removed manually, or the entire operation can be performed automatically. Many features and options allow a fabricator to choose the best saw for the application.

If close tolerances, .005 inch or less, and finish are not primary in an application, then a band saw is probably the most economical saw selection.

Vertical Saws

A vertical band saw is similar to a horizontal band saw in that a continuous loop blade revolves

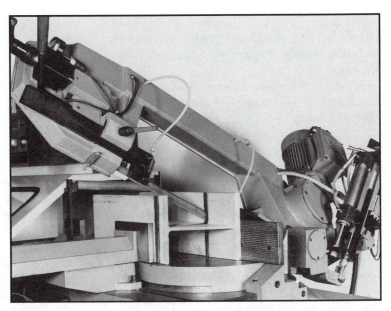

Figure 1-3. Shown here is one type of pivot head horizontal band saw that can be operated manually, semiautomatically, or automatically.

on two or more wheels to perform the cutting. The primary difference is that the blade revolves on a vertical, rather than horizontal, cutting plane.

This type of saw design is often selected because of its ability to cut circular patterns or intricate contours. To perform the cut on this type of saw, either the head frame travels on a horizontal plane through the piece, or the piece is indexed through the blade.

Vertical saws with traveling head frames are available with head frames that can be adjusted to tilt while being indexed through the part for miter cuts. The table tilts for miter cutting on vertical saws with stationary heads.

Vertical saws with a stationary head are usually classified by size as indicated by the distance between the blade and the saw frame. This distance is referred to as the **throat depth**.

Most stationary head vertical saws are furnished with a blade welder so that continuous blade loops can be fabricated on the spot. Welders are required when there is a need to cut only the inside of a part, leaving the outside section intact. This type of internal cut is accomplished by drilling an appropriately placed hole, threading a blade through the hole, and welding the blade together.

A welder also enables the vertical saw user to buy blades on rolls instead of prewelded, making blades as needed.

Cutting or trimming intricate contours is another feature of this machine. Given the variety of different materials that can be cut on this type of saw, a range of blade widths usually exists for mounting on the saw. Blade speeds are variable and adjustable for different cutting requirements.

The limiting factor on the size of the part that can be cut is usually the throat depth.

Another favorable characteristic of a vertical band saw is the comfortable working height of the table. It usually stands about 40 inches from the ground so that the operator can hold and see the work being performed at a convenient height. This ergonomic design feature is important for minimizing operator fatigue, thereby reducing scrap parts.

The second popular style of vertical band saw features a head frame that is driven through the piece being cut. This machine cuts the same type of material as a horizontal machine, yet gives the fabricator quick and easy mitering and comfortable working height and consumes less floor space than a horizontal saw of comparable capacities.

Summary

Today's fabricator has more sawing machine choices than ever before: cold saw, horizontal band saw, and fixed and traveling head vertical saws. Each type can be modified to enhance performance for specific job requirements.

Selecting the best cutting technology requires careful assessment of all the metal cutting resources available. To minimize risk and optimize cutting performance when searching for a metal cutting saw, it is best to deal with an established, reputable supplier. The supplier should have local factory-trained representation and distribution to provide technical knowledge and support.

The same criteria should be used to determine a blade supplier — a crucial element in cutting performance.

Finally, to be truly successful in applying current metal cutting sawing technology, a commitment must be made to educate and continuously train saw operators to maintain peak cutting performance. The old rule of thumb still applies: a saw is only as good as the blade it uses and the expertise of the operator.

Factors affecting band saw cutting performance: Making your sawing operation a profit-making function

Traditionally, most people in the metal forming and fabricating industry have regarded the sawing operation as a necessary evil. The principles of band saw cutting generally are not widely known. The resulting approach too frequently has been, "Just stick the material in the machine and chop it off."

As knowledge of band saw cutting increases, wise shop owners are beginning to realize that sawing is a legitimate operation.

Under the right conditions, in-house sawing has the potential of actually making money. However, a foundation consisting of certain factors must be laid:

1. A knowledge of the elements affecting the physical operation of cutting — such as blade speed, material size and composition, and feed rate and pressure

2. The ability to maximize the efficiency of band saw cutting in terms of time, accuracy, and blade life

3. The selection of a saw which will provide superior performance in terms of unit cost, overhead cost, and long-range profitability

This article gives practical information on factors that affect band saw cutting performance. Obviously, every topic relevant to band saw cutting cannot be addressed in one article, and further study is encouraged.

Material Composition

As the material machinability lowers, so does the cutting rate. For example, stainless steel is slower to cut than C1212, which in turn is slower than B1113.

Surface conditions also affect the cutting rate. If some places on the surface or in the material are hard, a slower blade speed will be required to prevent blade damage. Tough or abrasive materials are harder to cut than their machinability rating indicates.

Material Size and Shape

Each blade configuration has an optimum width of material to be cut. Below this width, tooth loading may become excessive, and the cutting rate must be reduced. When the material is wider than the optimum width, blade control begins to diminish.

For example, a band saw blade 1 inch wide by .035 inch thick would successfully cut material with an optimum width between 4 and 5 inches. However, a blade 1.25 inches wide by .042 inch thick has optimum cutting in stock which is about 6 inches wide. This is because the heavier blade has nearly twice the beam strength, which allows higher pressure and straighter cutting in heavier material.

Since the blade "sees" only the material actually being cut, the shape of the stock being cut will also affect cutting speeds, particularly if the piece is excessively wide or if it varies in the dimensions being cut.

Cutting tubing presents special problems. For instance, the blade must enter the material twice, and maintaining adequate cutting fluid flow on the blade as it enters the second side is nearly impossible.

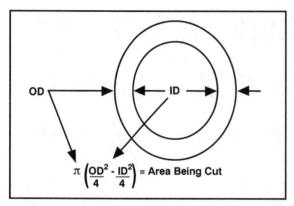

Figure 2-1. As tube wall thickness increases, the tubing begins to resemble more and more closely a solid in terms of cutting speed.

Thus, whenever the inside diameter (ID) begins to approach 50 percent or less of the outside diameter (OD), it is best for practical purposes to treat the material as a solid. In other words, as wall thickness increases, the tubing begins to resemble more closely a solid in terms of cutting speed (see **Figure 2-1**).

Guide Spacing

The rigidity of the blade is a function of guide spacing, with rigidity being reduced to the third power as the distance between the guides increases.

For example, with guides spaced 2 inches apart, blade deflection might be approximately .02 inch. Under the same conditions, but with the guides spaced at 4 inches apart, blade deflection would be approximately .16 (.02 x 8) inch.

A simplified formula is:

$$Y \max = \frac{1WL^3}{48 \, EI}$$

where: Y = blade deflection
W = load on blade
L = spacing of guides
E = modulus of elasticity
I = moment of inertia

This is a simplified version of the formula because it does not consider band tension or guide design. It is important to recognize, for

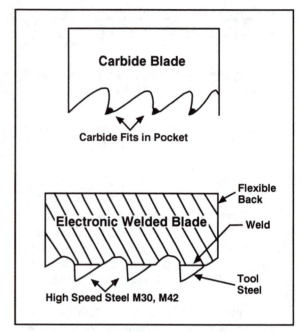

Figure 2-2. Bimetal blades usually consist of a tool steel electron beam welded to a tough backer material.

example, that rollers are not considered anchored supports. A more complete formula is included in *Roark's Formulas for Stress and Strain.*[1]

The greater the distance between the guides, the greater the probability of a crooked cut. The solution is to reduce cutting pressure. However, if the material is hard or tough, cutting may stop altogether. Thus, when cutting wide stock, a compromise between too much and too little cutting pressure must be found. Trial and error may be the only satisfactory method.

Blade Selection

Many types of blade materials are used, ranging from carbon to carbide. Each specific blade material has its own application. Carbon blades, both hardback and flexback, generally cannot be recommended for production cutting because the blades have poor resistance to heat and abrasion. However, certain applications may exist where a hardened carbon blade may be used for cost-effectiveness.

[1]*Warren C. Young, Roark's Formulas for Stress and Strain (New York: McGraw-Hill Book Company, 1989).*

All-high-speed blades, popular a few years ago, can be replaced by bimetal blades. Bimetal blades come in many configurations. However, they generally consist of a tool steel (M30 or M42) electron beam-welded to a tough backer material (see **Figure 2-2**). Many variations have been made on this construction to provide high resistance to heat or shock.

The bimetal blade has the greatest versatility and use in the metal sawing business. Additionally, other blades are available for special applications. For example, carbide-tipped blades (see Figure 2-2) permit cutting of extremely abrasive or hard materials. All blades have their particular advantages.

In the right application, carbide blades with their ground teeth will provide a better finish and higher production rates than more conventional sawing methods.

Tooth Form and Spacing

The selection of a tooth form is generally determined by the material to be cut. Three general factors must be considered:

1. **Tooth form** — the style or shape of the teeth
2. **Tooth spacing** — the number of teeth to the inch
3. **Tooth set** — provides clearance for the body of the blade

In general, a coarse, hook-tooth blade is the most efficient in materials such as mild steel and aluminum. For wide cuts, a skip-tooth blade is effective, since it simply reduces the number of teeth per inch.

The standard-tooth blade is, of course, a blade for general applications or for cutting a variety of materials. It is also particularly useful for cutting fragile materials, such as castings and brass.

These three styles of teeth are shown in **Figure 2-3**.

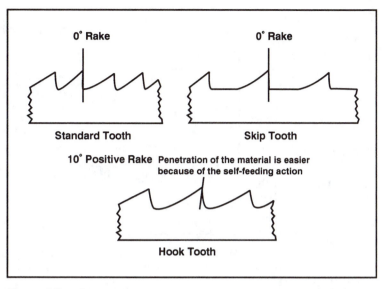

Figure 2-3. Three styles of teeth are: standard tooth, skip tooth, and hook tooth.

Hammer Set

The hammer set (**see Figure 2-4**) changes the rake angle and the side profile. The greater the rake angle, the easier it is for the blade to penetrate the material. The penetration of the material is due to the self-feeding action of the rake angle. Hammer setting the side changes the tooth cutting edge from the same angle as the set to a smaller angle. This helps the blade cut straighter.

The larger the rake angle, the greater the self-feeding action of the blade. This self-feeding lowers the cutting pressure, but the teeth are more fragile.

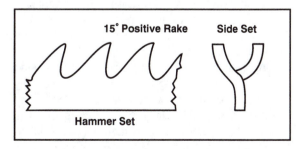

Figure 2-4. The hammer set changes the rake angle and the side profile. The greater the rake angle, the easier it is for the blade to penetrate the material.

Types of Blades

Triple Chip Grind on Carbide Blades. The triple chip grind consists of high teeth, low teeth, and wide teeth. The high tooth cuts a small chip in the center of the cut. The wide tooth cuts both edges and widens the cut, and cuts on both sides at the same time. It prevents the blade from binding in the cut.

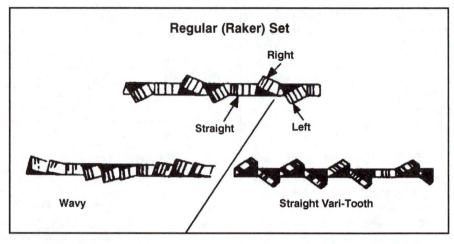

Figure 2-5. On bimetal or carbon blades, set prevents the blade from binding in the cut. It may be either a regular (raker) set, wavy set, or variable pitch.

On bimetal or carbon blades, set prevents the blade from binding in the cut. It may be either a **regular set** (also called a **raker set)**, **wavy set**, or **variable pitch** (see **Figure 2-5**).

The regular or raker set is most common and consists of a pattern of one tooth to the left, one to the right, and one (the raker) which is straight, or unset. This type of set is generally used on uniform-size material and for contour cutting.

Wavy set has groups of teeth set alternately to the right and left, forming a wave-like pattern. This reduces the stress on each individual tooth, making it suitable for cutting thin materials or a variety of materials with which blade changing is impractical. Wavy set is often used when tooth breakage is a problem.

Today, however, the variable pitch has replaced most of the wavy tooth applications. When this tooth enters the material, the right tooth takes a larger bite on the side.

Stepped Backed Blades. Stepped or ground backed blades (see **Figure 2-6**) are a relatively new development for metal band sawing. They are designed specifically for the cutting of large cross-sectional sizes or hard materials. The blade tends not to perform well on servo-controlled or constant feed rate band saws.

Wavy Tooth. With a wavy-tooth blade, the changing height of the tips is an attempt to improve cutting in the same manner as the stepped backed blade (see **Figure 2-7**).

Tooth pitch, or spacing, is generally determined by the material and its thinness in cross section. It is generally specified in "teeth per inch."

Vari-Pitch Teeth. A relatively new development is blades with variable tooth spacing (see **Figure 2-8**). On blades of this type, the tooth spacing might, for example, vary from 3 to 6 teeth per inch on a particular blade. On a less coarse tooth blade, it might vary from 6 to 10 teeth per inch. The purpose of this type of tooth spacing is to prevent vibration.

When cutting narrow shapes, more teeth per inch are required to prevent damaging the blade. Wider shapes require a coarse blade with fewer teeth per inch.

Blade Sharpness

A dull blade will cause problems, which is no surprise. However, a very sharp blade can also be a source of difficulty — vibration.

When a very sharp point enters the material, it immediately begins to dig itself into the material. At some point, it gets in too deep and "bounces" up. The next tooth does the same thing, and the result, of course, is vibration. Excessive vibration reduces blade life and also causes excessive wear on other parts of the saw.

As the blade begins to dull just slightly, the points of the teeth stop digging in and the vibration stops. Now, the teeth must be pushed into the material by the saw, permitting proper cutting pressure to be applied.

How to "Break In" Blades

The honing process is best accomplished by careful breaking in of the new blade immediately after installation, as follows:

1. Set blade speed according to material type and size

2. Reduce the cutting pressure on the blade to the minimum required to achieve cutting

3. Gradually increase the cutting rate until the desired square inches per minute is achieved

Some blade manufacturers actually sandblast their blades to remove the very sharp points. This may be an advantage only in situations involving inexpert saw operators and difficult materials. Careful break-in of a new blade is the best method of obtaining the maximum blade life.

A dull blade cannot be expected to cut straight. As an example, picture a 10 pitch blade with .001 flat on each tooth (generally smaller than a human eye can detect). When cutting a piece 4 inches wide, 40 teeth would be engaged in the material at one time. That is a total of .040 flat on the point.

In addition, a dull blade does not cut efficiently. As the blade gets dull, it penetrates more slowly and generates more heat. The additional heat tends to dull the blade more quickly. The blade becomes duller still, generates even more heat, and so on. Soon, the teeth will fail and the blade will not cut at all, or it will make crooked cuts.

Since a dull tooth cannot be detected by the naked eye, cutting time is the most reliable indication of a dull blade. Typically, as a blade begins to dull, the cutting time will begin to show a significant increase.

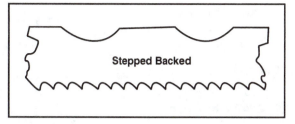

Figure 2-6. Stepped or ground backed blades are a relatively new development for metal band sawing. They are designed for cutting large cross-sectional sizes or hard materials.

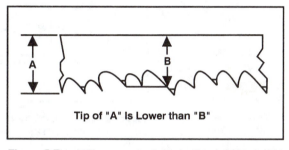

Figure 2-7. With a wavy-tooth blade, the changing height of the tips is an attempt to improve cutting in the same manner as the stepped back blade.

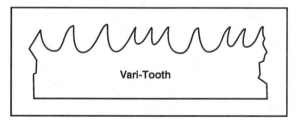

Figure 2-8. Another relatively new development is blades with variable tooth spacing. The purpose of this type of tooth spacing is to prevent vibration.

It is possible, but not economical, to leave the blade on until cutting time has increased to two or even three times the normal time. However, maximum efficiency and straight cutting require that the blade be changed as soon as the dulling begins to become apparent.

Note that if a blade is too dull to cut stainless or similar materials efficiently, it may still be satisfactory to use in mild steel. However, a blade which is too dull for mild steel will not be satisfactory in aluminum.

Blade Speed and Feed Rate (Traversing Rate)

Blade speed is generally limited by vibration and by the ability to keep the blade sufficiently cool to avoid dulling the teeth. A blade which is running fast and taking a very shallow cut dulls quickly because the tips of the teeth overheat from the rubbing action.

If, however, the blade teeth are forced deeper into the material, the blade is less sensitive to heat because the teeth are cutting more and rubbing less. This increased pressure may also prevent vibration. Thus, up to a point, a higher pressure on the blade may actually permit higher blade speeds.

When using a sharp tooth with a .0002 radius on the tip, applying only enough force to cause penetration of .0002, the tooth will not penetrate and cut. If, however, enough force is applied to cause penetration of .001, the tooth still has .0008 of a sharp edge with which to cut.

This is similar to the "dull tip effect" observed frequently in lathe and milling operations. When making a finish cut with a dull tool, a fine adjustment may make no cut at all, but an additional fine adjustment causes the tool to dig in deeply.

If, on the other hand, too much penetrating force is applied, the teeth will be ripped out of the blade. The maximum feed rate is determined by the saw, material size, material shape, guide spacing, cutting fluid, and the size and shape of the teeth. The greater the blade speed, the greater the feed rate can be, up to the limits imposed by the factors just discussed.

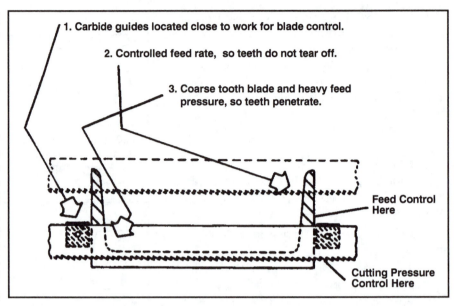

1. Carbide guides located close to work for blade control.

2. Controlled feed rate, so teeth do not tear off.

3. Coarse tooth blade and heavy feed pressure, so teeth penetrate.

Feed Control Here

Cutting Pressure Control Here

Figure 2-9. For each blade and material being cut, there is an optimum balance between blade speed and feed rate. Three recommendations are illustrated here.

Thus, for each blade and material being cut, there is an optimum balance between blade speed and feed rate. This rate gives maximum blade life and most satisfactory cutting. In general, the following are recommended (see **Figure 2-9**):

1. Coarse tooth blade so that each tooth has adequate force on it

2. Guides set close to the work to permit relatively heavy feed pressure and still control the blade

3. Carefully controlled feed rate to prevent the teeth from tearing out

Feed Rate or Pressure Control System

The most efficient cutting is accomplished by the proper balance between cutting pressure and feed rate (see **Figure 2-10**).

Soft, low-strength materials present different difficulties than hard, high-strength materials. In soft, low-strength material, pulling the teeth off the blade is unlikely, but over-filling the gullet may occur.

With high-strength material, pulling the teeth off the blade is a major problem. Carbide blades present other difficulties because of their shock sensitivity and sensitivity to pulling the teeth off. The feed rate must be set right so the teeth are not overstressed.

Feed Rate System (Traversing Rate)

Feed speed (traversing rate) is used to maintain a uniform speed through the material. The pressure on the saw teeth will vary during the cut. Advantages are:

1. Uniform chip thickness.

2. As the blade teeth get dull, the chip thickness will remain constant.

3. If the material work-hardens, the blade will be forced into the material.

4. Cutting time remains constant.

Disadvantages are:

1. Slower cutting time in nonuniform cross sections.

2. As the blade teeth get dull, the blade may cut crooked.

3. When the blade teeth are too dull to cut, the blade will stall and slip on the wheel.

4. Each different width material will require a different traversing rate. The operator must make the change, or the teeth may be overloaded.

It is best to have a "maximum-force-allowed" safety device on traversing rate saws.

Cutting Pressure System

Cutting pressure systems are used to maintain the best cutting rate in all shapes and for easy setups. However, the feed rate varies as the cross section varies.

Advantages are:

1. Gullet loads are maintained in a more constant manner.

2. Best cutting rates in shapes.

3. Cutting rate slows as the blade dulls, thereby maintaining a straight cut.

4. Ease of setup.

5. Changing the width of the material does not require a change in cutting pressure.

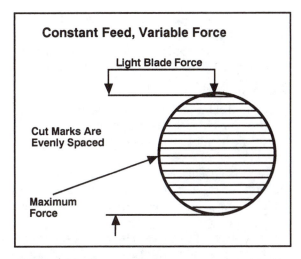

Figure 2-10. The most efficient cutting is accomplished by the proper balance between cutting pressure and feed rate. Slow entry (at top) means light blade force, and that may dull the blade in work-hardening material or in bars with hard or abrasive scale. In the wide section, the blade gullets may be overfilled, stripping the saw teeth out, or the blade may stall.

6. As the material gets wider, the traversing rate of the saw slows, but the square inches cut per minute remains the same.

Disadvantages are:

1. In thin sections, the chip load may be too large, and the teeth may pull out.

2. In work hardening material, the saw teeth may quit penetrating, and the material may work harden under the teeth. The saw will stop cutting.

3. Cutting time will slow as the blade becomes dull.

4. Different tooth configurations may require a different pressure.

It is best to have a maximum traversing speed adjustment with the cutting pressure control (see **Figure 2-11**).

Blade Tension

Blade tension is an important factor in straight cutting. Adequate tension prevents the center of the blade from being deflected to the side, causing a crooked cut. It also prevents the blade from achieving reduced penetration of the teeth in the center of the cut.

From the cutting standpoint, the more tension, the better. The limiting factor is blade strength.

Cutting Fluid

Cutting fluid is so important it cannot be over-stressed. A high-quality cutting fluid in a band saw is one of the most important factors in straight cutting.

The cutting fluid keeps the blade teeth cool; prevents the chips from welding to the tooth; and lubricates the chips, allowing them to move easily through the cut.

If the cutting fluid is unable to cool the blade teeth, they will soften and become dull. If the cutting fluid is distributed to only one side of the blade, the opposite side becomes dull. This causes the blade to move toward the side which has the most cutting fluid, and the cut becomes crooked.

In comparison to milling, sawing has much less room for the chip. The chip must lodge in a small place between the teeth and be carried smoothly out of the cut. Without proper cutting fluid, one of two things will happen.

First, the chip may become welded to the tooth. This will change the form of the tooth, which, in turn, changes the amount of force required for the blade to cut. The result is an unbalanced blade which will produce a crooked cut.

The second possibility is that the chip will wedge in the cut. Since the chip is work-hardened and harder than the stock from which it came, the blade will cut into the stock beside the chip. Again, the result is a crooked cut and a dull blade.

In selecting a cutting fluid, pick one which is of high quality. Avoid thinly-mixed soluble oils. Some of the new synthetic oils are highly satisfactory in difficult operations.

If optimum cutting and blade life are the desired result, before selecting a cutting fluid and mixture for a saw, ask yourself if you would tap this material with this fluid.

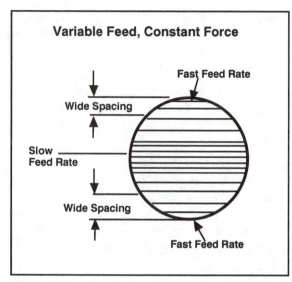

Figure 2-11. It is best to have a maximum traversing speed adjustment with the cutting pressure control. As shown here, in the top and bottom section, the saw teeth may penetrate too deeply, overloading the saw teeth and causing them to pull out.

Saw Design and Construction

Satisfactory and profitable cutting performance is determined by a variety of factors, most of which involve the design and construction of the saw.

The first objective of proper saw design is straight cutting, because this permits work to be done with a minimum of reprocessing, material waste, and rejects. Straight cutting is so important to profits that it almost goes without further comment.

The second objective is efficient use of blades. To grasp the importance of this, compare the difference between using one electron beam-welded blade costing $25 for one day and using the blade for two days. On the basis of a five-day week, 50 weeks per year, a machine which uses one blade per day will require $6,250 in blades per year. However, a machine which will extend the life of the blade to two days will require only $3,125 in blades.

Over a period of three years, savings in blades alone will pay for a $10,000 saw. This does not even take into account such factors as reduced labor time, a lower reject rate, or less material waste due to dull blades.

Another objective of good saw design is maximum production efficiency, which includes the greatest reliability, ease of adjustment and repair, and the best possible return on investment.

Precision sawing adds value for end users: How to precision cut plate and extrusions for a profit

Precision cutting of metal has one purpose: to eliminate machining subsequent to sawing, thereby reducing the ultimate cost of parts to the end user. Precision cutting is becoming more commonplace — and more necessary — because of a combination of technological and economic forces.

Economics and Marketing

Fifteen years ago, a number of systems were available for cutting both plate and extrusions to what today would be considered open tolerances. The purpose of this equipment was to cut a full-size plate or extrusion into sections small enough to be easily handled by the end user. This equipment was used by original material manufacturers as well as by metal-distributing companies.

From another perspective, this kind of equipment simply cut bulk-sale material for the sake of convenience. No attempt was made to saw the part to the dimensions customers wanted. Instead, customers processed the material to the desired size.

As a result, customers required parts to be cut oversize by $\frac{1}{16}$ or $\frac{1}{32}$ inch to allow milling. In fact, many material manufacturers and distributors would add an extra dimension on the customer's already oversize order to ensure that parts were never undersize.

This was the situation until about 15 years ago, when the effort was first made to design and build sawing systems that could cut material to tolerances precise enough to eliminate purposeful over-sizing and subsequent machining. Over the past decade, such equipment has become sophisticated, available, and necessary for economic survival.

In the Los Angeles area, for example, about 50 precision metal-cutting saws are now in use in the metal-distributing network. Companies simply must have such equipment to be competitive. The economic incentive toward precision cutting is paramount. As margins on bulk material have declined, metal-distributing companies and material manufacturers have had to incorporate value-added processing.

Precision sawing fits this need well, for both supplier and user. The parts producer gains additional revenue, while the customer gets a part that requires no subsequent machining and thus reduces costs.

Obviously, this technological shift alters sales representatives' roles drastically. In the days of open tolerances, sales people sold a commodity. They visited the purchasing agent, determined what material the agent wanted and in what size or shape, and placed the order. There was no technical discussion except about the type of material.

Precision cutting, though, makes the sales representatives marketers of precision parts. Now, they must approach the engineering or manufacturing department, determine their requirements in detail, and demonstrate how their parts fit the need. The sales force must be technically oriented so that they can talk meaningfully with engineers about such topics as tolerances and surface finishes.

Measurement and Terminology

Five dimension measurements apply to the cutting of precision parts. We will look at each one in turn.

Straightness. The straightness of a processed edge is defined as the distance between two parallel planes within which all points on a cut edge lie. Normally, straightness is measured by comparing the cut edge with a "straight edge" or flat surface by means of visual inspection, a feeler gauge, or a dial indicator.

The straightness of a sawed edge can be adversely affected by residual stress in the material. When the standards of squareness and parallelism are attended to, the degree of straightness is implied.

Parallelism. There is a difference between parallelism and straightness. Parallelism usually refers to the relationship of two opposite sawed edges, while straightness refers only to one edge.

Parallelism can, however, refer to the relationship of the top and bottom sides of the part. In this case, the parallelism tolerance zone is defined as the distance between two parallel planes that establish the maximum and the minimum allowable distances of one sawed edge from the parallel plane formed by the opposite sawed edge.

Parallelism is measured with calipers or with a flat plate and a dial indicator. Since two sides may be parallel but not straight, parallelism is best measured on a flat surface. Be sure, too, to check the straightness of the edge lying on the flat surface, since it can affect parallelism.

The measurement process involves two steps:

1. Check both ends and intermediate points of the sawed part with calipers or a micrometer.

2. Place the sawed plate on edge on a flat surface and check various points with a height gauge. Alternatively, compare the surface height to a standard height of gauge blocks with a dial indicator.

Squareness or Perpendicularity. Since squareness probably causes more confusion than any other tolerance requirement, let us try to simplify it. The squareness of a sawed part is defined as the distance between two parallel planes perpendicular to the datum plane formed by the referenced surface (see **Figure 3-1**). Squareness tolerance may be specified for vertical and/or horizontal edges.

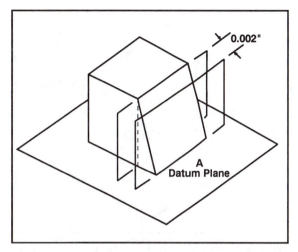

Figure 3-1. Vertical squareness is measured by determining the distance between the two parallel planes perpendicular to the datum plane formed by the reference surface.

Squareness tolerances typically determine the maximum deviation of the entire length of one edge or side to the plane formed by the referenced surface. However, care must be taken to understand what the allowable tolerance refers to.

A tolerance specification may dictate the allowable deviation over the entire length of two measured surfaces, or it may refer to the allowable deviation per inch from the square corner. The difference will significantly affect the care with which the saw operator must run the precision saw.

Squareness tolerance specifications must state clearly how squareness is defined and/or measured. For example, a piece measuring 10 inches by 24 inches that is cut to squareness tolerances of ±0.005 inch requires a higher degree of squareness than a piece measuring 1 inch by 2 inches and cut to the same tolerance.

Squareness can be checked in three ways:

1. With a precision machinist square or precision square gauge blocks, measure deviation at all points with a feeler gauge.

2. Place the piece on a flat surface and use a sliding vertical dial indicator squareness gauge to measure deviation from top to bottom.

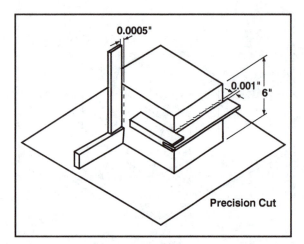

Figure 3-2. This precision-cut part shows the squareness tolerances achievable with today's equipment.

Horizontal Squareness ....±0.002 inch   (per inch measured from a square corner)

Vertical
Squareness ....±0.00075 inch
    (per inch of thickness measured vertically
             from bottom of plate)

Straightness.............................±0.002 inch   (per foot)
Parallelism ....±0.002 inch   (per foot)
Surface Finish ....±8-32 microinch (RMS)   (with precision-ground carbide-tipped blade)

Figure 3-3. The dimensional tolerances of precision sawing are shown here.

3. If the piece is a rectangle or a square, determine the difference between diagonal measurements. A truly square piece will have diagonals of equal length. Since a small burr can greatly affect dimensional characteristics, this method should be used only on large pieces not easily measured by one of the two previous methods.

Surface Finish. Surface finish is evaluated at right angles to the surface. Over a given sampling length, an imaginary centerline is passed through the section, and the average departure of the profile from this centerline is determined. The centerline is located so that the sum of the areas enclosed by the profile above the centerline equals the sum of the areas enclosed below.

Surface roughness is usually measured with a device called a profilometer or by comparing the sawed surface with a set of standard surface finish samples called a **surface finish comparator**.

The smaller the microinch number in measuring surface finish, the smoother the finish. A precision sawing system can produce surface finishes much finer than 32 microinches. By comparison, a milling machine usually produces a surface finish between 32 and 64 microinches.

Surface finish can be affected by such factors as cutting speed, the use of a blade with proper diameter and tooth configuration for the alloy,

metal thickness, proper application and consistency of the cooling lubricant, and, obviously, saw blade condition.

Flatness. The flatness tolerance of a surface is defined as the distance between two parallel planes that enclose the surface being measured. Flatness can be controlled by sawing only when six-sided sawing is required. Otherwise, flatness is a function of the plate being cut.

Sawing Equipment Capabilities

The difference in tolerances between standard sawing equipment and a precision sawing system are significant (see **Figure 3-2**). The table in **Figure 3-3** demonstrates these differences in terms of the tolerance dimensions achievable with modern precision-sawing equipment.

Marketing Precision-Cut Parts

Precision sawing provides the supplier with a business opportunity that requires a new marketing approach. A number of important areas need to be considered to develop a coherent, effective marketing campaign.

New Business Opportunity. You, the supplier, have a completely new product to offer — not plate in a different form, but a manufactured part. This new product becomes so integral to your customer's manufacturing process that it

Aerospace	Electronics	Light Manufacturing	Medium Manufacturing
Missiles	Guidance Systems	Appliances	Baggage-Handling Systems
Satellites	Radar Systems	Film-Processing Equipment	Conveyors
Aircraft	Microwave Systems	Office Equipment	Materials-Handling Equipment
Engines	Recording Equipment	Medical Test Equipment	Machine Shops
Launchers	Antennae	Laboratory Equipment	Custom Fabricators
	Control Panels	Computers	Heat Exchangers
	Telecommunications	Printers	Small Machine Shops
	Cabinets and Enclosures	Cryogenics Apparatus	Food-Processing Equipment
	Test Equipment	Heating and Air Conditioning	Packaging Equipment
	Electronic Manufacturing	Small Machine Shops	

Figure 3-4. Listed here are potential customers for precision parts.

affects tooling and manufacturing philosophy, can influence design, and will cut costs.

Precision parts offer better margins than do bare metal sales. The value-added nature of precision parts lessens competitive pricing pressures, and precision parts increase the customer's dependence on you as a supplier.

The potential customer base is now much larger, and it involves a different group of decision-makers, such as production supervisors, manufacturing engineers, shop managers, and product designers. To approach these people successfully, you will need to use a new product approach with the correct sales support.

Product literature, price sheets, inside sales support, training of field sales representatives, precision part samples, and testimonials from customers will provide sales support. Changes in plant operations will be likely to include material handling, inspection, and shop order systems.

Identifying the Market. The easiest market to approach is comprised of the customers who are already doing business with you. Review your customer lists and talk to the largest buyers first about the new way you can help them cut costs. Since you already have an established relationship with current customers, you will be working from a base of credibility.

Precision sawing also opens a new, untapped market. Occasional buyers who have not been sig-

nificant customers become sales prospects. Since precision parts offer a higher profit level than bare metal, a sales call is now worth your time.

In addition, even small orders are profitable because the pricing system includes a special setup charge and scrap rate. Once the customer relationship is established, subsequent small orders can be handled over the phone.

Finally, there are totally new customers. The table in **Figure 3-4** lists the industry types and products that use precision-sawed parts. All are potential customers for value-added processing.

Customer Contact. Decisions about precision sawing are made by technical people, not by the purchasing agent. Thus, your sales strategy must include contact with technical staff, typically at several levels in the decision-making hierarchy.

Manufacturing engineers and production supervisors are always looking for ways to cut costs and improve production rates. Your sales task is to show them how precision sawing will help accomplish one or both goals.

Become familiar with the customer's product, and identify the processes being used to make parts. If that processing is being done at the customer's plant, look for the scrap or remnant pile.

Remnants typically represent a substantial hidden expense that never enters the cost system. If the customer buys parts cut to size, find out who does the processing, what the cost is, and whether there have been problems.

If possible, try to get the customer to talk to you directly about costs, then develop a proposal or cost comparison on a specific application to show how precision sawing can save money.

A good proposal requires good information. You will need to determine the alloys used, current sizing costs, dimensions, tolerances, methods of checking tolerances and dimensions, edge finish requirements, and the permissibility of burrs. If possible, obtain a drawing of the part.

Besides costs, the proposal should cover the other benefits delivered by precision sawing. Precision sawing frees machine tools for other operations, simplifies production scheduling, allows deliveries to be planned to minimize finished parts inventory, reduces scrap, and prevents production interruptions, since emergency orders for parts can be handled promptly.

Systems and Procedures. Precision sawing is usually priced by either an individual job cost study with machine time input or a pricing table based on material thickness, length of cut, and degree of precision.

The individual job system is based on an esti-mate of actual costs for each application, including an analysis of the cutting process and cost/sell figures (such as energy, maintenance, labor, blade sharpening, plant burden, etc.). Hourly cost is totaled, then marked up to the required profit level to give a retail price per hour of sawing time. An individual job is priced by estimating material handling time plus cutting cycle time.

The individual job system is accurate, but a large volume of inquiries makes it cumbersome. It is, however, worth using for very large single projects or in tight competitive situations.

The standard price chart is simpler and more common. This system establishes three levels of sawing accuracy — open tolerance cutting, close tolerance cutting, and precision cutting —with price levels for each.

Conclusion

Precision sawing systems, combined with a thorough understanding of machine capabilities and tolerances, offer metal fabricators a marketing opportunity that can lead to improved profitability. The marketplace for finished parts is large and growing, and companies can profit by adding service and value for their customers.

Selecting and justifying a laser cutting system: Examining the benefits of lasers

The laser has achieved wide acceptance in manufacturing because it provides benefits that enhance a company's ability to compete in today's marketplace.

This article reviews the features and benefits of laser cutting machines and how these benefits can be used to generate a justification. Machine and operation costs are discussed, and a list is given of some of the questions that should be asked before a laser is purchased.

Since original equipment manufacturers (OEMs) have different requirements than contract shops, the article discusses areas in which both types of companies can expect to produce a justification for a laser cutting machine.

Setting Goals

The first question that needs to be addressed is, "Why a laser?" Categorizing the laser is difficult because it offers so much flexibility, but it is important to attach some expected benefits to the machine. The question "Why a laser?" forces an examination of the problem areas in a manufacturing environment that are to be addressed with a laser cutting system.

In some instances, a laser may produce im-

proved efficiencies under existing manufacturing conditions, but, in other cases, the current production models may have to be altered to take advantage of the laser system's abilities.

For example, if a company is producing small volumes of parts, the laser cutting system may be used to reduce setup and secondary operations. If a company is producing large quantities of parts, the laser might be considered for reduction of production lot sizes so that the benefits of Just-In-Time (JIT) manufacturing can be realized.

After a set of goals is outlined, a company is then able to match the capabilities of the laser system to its requirements.

Benefits of Laser Cutting Systems

Many advertisements and articles have extolled the advantages of laser cutting machines. In some cases, the improvements in productivity are so overwhelming that a justification is easy. In other cases, the benefits of the laser are less obvious.

The following is a review of the advantages of laser cutting compared to conventional sheet metal fabricating processes. Every advantage listed here will not apply in every case. Instead, this addresses a typical set of conditions in most sheet metal shops and departments. The laser offers:

1. Reduced setup time.

2. No tooling cost.

3. High cutting rates for most material.

4. No secondary deburring of laser cut parts.

5. Cutting of metals and non-metals.

6. Cutting of a range of material thicknesses.

7. Production of parts that cannot be made any other way.

8. Cutting details in formed parts and tubing.

9. Better accuracy than most other processes.

The following sections expand on each of these benefits.

Reduced Setup Time

Reduced setup time has always been a strong selling point for the laser cutting machines. It is not unusual for a laser to be set up in five minutes, which makes the production of small quantities cost-effective.

When compared to a turret punch press, the laser offers faster changeover time between jobs. However, the laser's advantage in setup time is offset on longer runs by the turret press's faster hole-making rate. For parts that have few holes, the laser is competitive for greater lot sizes. For very hole-intensive parts, the turret press quickly overcomes the setup time deficit.

The exact quantity of parts necessary for the turret to be more efficient varies.

The two graphs in **Figure 4-1** show parts run on a laser and a turret press and the relationship of setup to runtime. In both instances, the laser takes less time to set up. This is shown where the lines intersect the time axis in Figure 4-1.

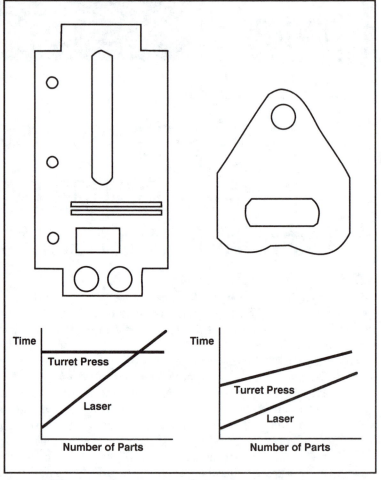

Figure 4-1. These graphs show the relationship of setup to runtime for parts made on a laser and a turret press.

For the first part, the turret is shown to make up the deficit in setup time more quickly than on the second part. This is due to the nature of the two parts. The graphs do show that on small lot sizes, the setup advantage of the laser will not be made up by the turret press.

No Tooling Cost

The laser uses focused light to vaporize and melt the material in place of tooling. The shape of the part is generated by moving the laser beam or the material along a preprogrammed path. Unlike other thermal processes such as plasma, small holes as well as the outside perimeter can be cut with the laser, which generates its own start hole.

Parts with unusual holes or patterns can be produced quickly because special tools are not needed. The laser beam does not need to be sharpened and does not wear, so high-strength steel and super alloys can be cut.

The costs associated with laser cutting include gases, optics, power, and other consumables, but these will be included in the hourly operating costs. The operating costs are fairly constant, and each part has to carry a share. With a laser, however, there is no large initial outlay for tooling that may become obsolete because of short product life or a part modification.

High Cutting Rates

Cutting rates for lasers depend on several factors, such as material type, thickness, and the geometry of the part. Machine configuration, laser output power, and the processing speed of the control also play a part in production rates. A table outlining linear cutting rates is shown in **Figure 4-2**.

It is important to realize that these rates are maximums. Most parts are produced at slower speeds because the geometry of the part requires the positioning system to generate small details that cannot be produced accurately at the listed speeds.

The question becomes, then, "What value do these cutting charts have?" The answer is that they have very limited value and only for gross overall comparisons between lasers of different powers.

Material	Thickness	Cutting Speed at 1,500 Watts	Cutting Speed at 1,000 Watts	Cutting Speed at 500 Watts
Mild Steel	0.062"	>325 IPM	~215 IPM	~150 IPM
Mild Steel	0.125"	~175 IPM	~117 IPM	~100 IPM
Mild Steel	0.250"	>60 IPM	~41 IPM	~25 IPM*
Mild Steel	0.375"	~50 IPM	~27 IPM	N/A*
Mild Steel	0.500"	~26 IPM	~14 IPM	N/A*
304 Stainless Steel	0.062"	>295 IPM	~185 IPM	~160 IPM
304 Stainless Steel	0.125"	~150 IPM	~95 IPM	~75 IPM
304 Stainless Steel	0.250"	>42 IPM	~26 IPM	N/A*
304 Stainless Steel	0.375"	>20 IPM	~12 IPM	N/A*
304 Stainless Steel	0.500"	~15 IPM	N/A	N/A*
High nickel steels cut very similar to stainless steels.				
Aluminum	0.050"	>175 IPM	~143 IPM	*
Aluminum	0.062"	>150 IPM	~85 IPM	*
Aluminum	0.125"	>40 IPM	~13 IPM	*
Aluminum	0.187"	>5 IPM	*	*

* A cut in this thickness of material may not be attainable, the cut quality may not be acceptable, or the speed of cut is below acceptable limits.

Figure 4-2. This table outlines linear cutting rates.

Machines from different suppliers produce parts at different rates, so several systems should be tested before a machine selection is made. Part quality can also be affected by the cutting rate, as noted in the graph in **Figure 4-3**.

No Secondary Deburring

Parts produced by the laser are flat and undistorted because the heat from the laser is very focused, and laser cutting is a noncontact process. A properly set up laser system will produce dross-free parts on most materials.

A laser will cut mild steel with no dross and no need to deburr the part. Stainless steel and aluminum up to 3⁄16 inch thick can be cut with no dross using either oxygen or inert gas as an assist. This allows a company to eliminate secondary operations and reduce Work-In-Process (WIP).

Cutting Metals and Nonmetals

The laser can cut composites, plastics, and wood, as well as steel, stainless steel, and aluminum. Tool steels such as A2 and nickel-based super alloys, which are difficult to punch, can be cut easily with a laser.

Cutting Various Material Thicknesses

A 1,500-watt laser can cut alloy steel from a few thousandths to ½ inch thick. The same laser can cut stainless steel to ⅜ inch thick. The laser is a convenient tool when a range of material thicknesses have to be processed.

Producing Difficult Parts

Often, instances occur when part configuration, material specification, or quality requirements do not allow production of a part with conventional tooling. The laser is often able to make parts that cannot be made any other way, and it does so efficiently and quickly.

Cutting Details in Formed Parts

Most laser systems have a programmable third axis that permits the processing of formed parts and square and rectangular tubing. The part can be mounted in a fixture on the laser system so that cutting can be done on the horizontal surface. This feature can be used to correct parts that need an additional hole after they have been formed.

On some parts, hole locations are very critical, and forming and welding make production in the flat very difficult. A laser system with a computer numerically-controlled (CNC) Z axis can be used to put holes in a part after it is formed and welded.

For companies that make enclosures with different front panels, the laser cutting machine can be used to customize standard boxes after they are formed to allow fast delivery of "specials."

The three-axis systems have limited capabilities for processing formed parts. If an application requires the trimming of formed parts, a five-axis

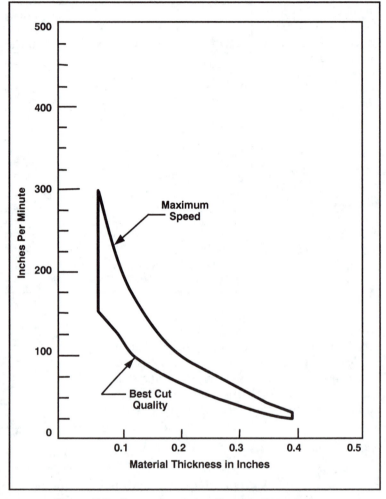

Figure 4-3. Part quality can be affected by the cutting rate.

system that has a moveable wrist should be considered. These machines offer the same X, Y, and Z axis motion as a flat cutter, but with the addition of an A and B axis of motion.

Five-axis cutting machines are used for trimming formed parts for the automotive and aerospace industries and offer advantages over conventional methods, especially for small lot sizes and preproduction runs.

The cost of a five-axis laser is usually two to three times greater than the three-axis systems discussed in this article.

High Accuracy

Accuracy of the laser depends on the type of machine, the material, and the environment of the shop. Small parts can be produced to accuracies of ±.002 inch.

If the application requires very tight tolerances, the laser system and the material would have to be maintained in a temperature-controlled environment. Better accuracy can also be produced with laser systems if the operator takes the time to adjust the beam offset after inspecting the first part.

Understanding how a manufacturer of a laser system specifies accuracy and repeatability is important because each company uses different criteria. Do not confuse a positioning accuracy specification with the ability of a machine to produce a part to that tolerance, because factors such as short-term laser stability will affect part accuracy.

These very small instabilities found in every laser have an effect on the surface finish and accuracy of the part.

JIT and Expanded Capabilities

All of these benefits can be grouped under two broad headings:

1. JIT manufacturing

2. Expanded capabilities

In most cases, laser cutting machines offer the most benefits when used for short to medium runs, usually in the 1 to 50 part range. The lack of tooling allows a shop to respond quickly to changing needs and product modifications. Reduced setup time and more efficient production of small quantities lead to less inventory and JIT manufacturing.

The expanded capabilities of the laser allow a company to process materials of all thicknesses and types, accurately and with little or no distortion. The term "expanded capabilities" includes the ability of a sheet metal shop, with a laser, to address traditional wire electrical discharge machining (EDM), machining, and plasma cutting applications.

Selecting the Right Equipment

Laser systems are available in many sizes and with different laser power. The right combination of power and work envelope depends on the material size and thickness of the parts that need to be produced. This step is important because the cost of the laser system is closely tied to the work envelope and laser power.

Following is an overview of available laser systems.

Machine design and configuration aside, two main work envelopes and two laser sizes are available on the U.S. market. The two main machine sheet capacities are 48 inch by 96 inch and 60 inch by 120 inch. Two of the most popular laser sizes are 1,000 and 1,500 watts.

Lasers of up to 3,000 watts are being offered by some machine suppliers, which is consistent with the trend toward higher power that has taken place over the past five years. Increases in laser output allow faster cutting in some metals and the ability to process thicker sections of other material. However, more powerful lasers also cost more to purchase and operate.

Work Envelope

Selecting the right work envelope is easy because current or future needs can be assessed. For example, if a large percentage of current production requires 120-inch blanks, the larger machine is appropriate. If a small percentage of work exceeds 96 inches, then the difference in cost of the two systems becomes a factor.

The different styles of machines also play a role in determining work envelopes. A fixed-beam, moving material type system with an open C frame can produce parts wider than the axis travel, and very long parts can be cut with automatic repositioning.

A full gantry or hybrid type system is limited to the distance between the vertical supports and the motion travel of the beam delivery system. It is important to make sure the work envelope is adequate with the pin table type machines because they may not be as adaptable as the fixed-beam type system.

Laser Output

Selecting the appropriate laser output for the application depends on the materials that need to be cut. If mild steel up to ¼ inch thick is all that will be processed, a 1,000-watt laser will be sufficient. If the application requires cutting large amounts of aluminum or stainless steel with an oxide-free edge, a 1,500-watt laser will be needed.

If the application is specific, tests on several manufacturers' systems will often determine the proper laser power. A job shop with no specific application should consider the 1,500-watt laser because it can offer greater capabilities and broader setup parameters than a 1,000-watt laser.

Since the cost of a machine depends on the size of the laser, a careful assessment of throughput versus the cost of the machine should be done before selecting a laser power. This will ensure that the cost advantage of the lower-powered machine can compensate for reduced production rates.

Machine Configuration

After the laser power and work envelope are selected, the features of the systems must be compared. Each machine design has features that offer advantages and disadvantages. Briefly, there are four main designs of laser systems:

1. Fixed beam, moving material
2. Fixed beam, moving table
3. Moving beam (full gantry)
4. Hybrid

A comparison of the different types of systems is needed to determine the right one for the application. Since several designs are available that produce similar results, take enough time to investigate each style thoroughly so that important features are not overlooked. Do not rule out a machine based on limited factual data.

Fixed Beam, Moving Material. This design is simple and reliable because of the small number of external optics, which do not move. The typical design is a C frame with the laser mount-ed on the frame or behind the motion system. The motion system is similar to a turret press which moves the material under the beam delivery system.

Finished parts are removed through doors in the table, and fume and dust collection is efficient.

Systems with lasers mounted on the frame usually require no foundation. The advantages of this design are minimal maintenance, stable beam delivery, and flexibility to handle large, oversized parts.

Fixed Beam, Moving Table. This is similar to the fixed beam, moving material design, but a "bed of nails" or honeycomb cutting table supports the material in place of a ball transfer table.

The advantages of the simple beam delivery and nonmoving optics are retained, but the pin table can limit the flexibility of this design. Fume collection is still efficient, and these systems are easy to maintain.

Moving Beam (Full Gantry). This design moves the beam delivery while the material is stationary on a pin or honeycomb table. This design is more complex and has from three to five moving external optics that direct the laser beam to the stationary workpiece. Alignment of the optics is more frequent and time-consuming with a moving beam design, especially when the beam path is very long.

This design is effective for very large, heavy work, and, on some systems, a second table can be added as a load/unload station. Dust and fume collection is more difficult because of the large area that has to be evacuated.

Hybrid. This design combines the fixed beam, moving table, and the full gantry system. Moving optics provide the Y-axis motion, and the moving pin table is used for the X axis of motion. This design limits the number of moving optics and the variations in the beam path to improve reliability and performance.

Small finished parts fall between the pins and are collected. Larger parts can be more time-consuming to remove. Fumes and dust can be collected more efficiently than on the full gantry system, but not as effectively as a fixed-beam design.

This description is simply an overview of the different designs and does not cover all the features of the machines. Many articles and papers have been written on the differences in machine design that cover the topic in greater detail.

Also, the manufacturers of the different types of machines can explain the benefits of each design. It is important to discuss requirements with several different manufacturers.

Other Factors

In addition to machine configuration, other factors must be considered before selecting a laser system supplier.

Training. Every laser supplier offers training when selling a system, and every customer should take advantage of the training offered. This seems like a common-sense statement, but, because of the size of a shop or other constraints, some customers do not take advantage of the training offered by a system manufacturer.

Training is offered either at a school for several customers or at the customer's facility. The good feature of off-site training is that the operator can focus on the task of learning the machine. The cost to a company in travel expenses and lost production by the employee must be considered.

On-site training may not be as effective because the operator is often distracted and unable to commit to the training full-time. On-site training may seem less expensive, but it can extend the learning curve so that any savings are questionable.

In any case, the cost of training must be considered when purchasing a laser system.

Programming the Laser. Most companies decide to program the laser with a computer-aided design/computer-aided manufacturing (CAD/CAM) system and only use the programming features of the control for minor corrections or in limited situations. Using off-line CAD/CAM allows the operator to concentrate on producing parts and maintaining the machine.

Most CNCs can be used to program the machine, and most have graphics and background programming features, but sometimes an operator can be distracted on the production floor. In this case, it may be more efficient to produce programs off-line.

The cost of a CAD/CAM system or of a post-processor for an existing programming system needs to be added to the cost of the laser system.

Special Environment for the Machine. Some laser systems require a foundation and special temperature and humidity considerations. Review the installation requirements to determine if any modifications have to be made to the area in which the laser will be placed. These modifications can add significant costs to the laser installation. Noncompliance could affect the machine warranty.

Fume and Dust Removal. Laser cutting machines require fume and dust collection systems. Some systems come with dust collection systems; other manufacturers offer them as options. A company with an existing collection system might be able to tie the laser into the current system.

The fume collection system must be capable of handling the material that will be cut. By-products from plastics, composites, and some metals need to be removed from the cutting area, and provisions must be made for this if the machine does not have adequate filtering systems.

Collecting fumes and dust from fixed-beam systems can be easier because a vacuum only has to be created around the cutting head. Moving beam machines require larger, more powerful vacuum systems because a larger area has to be evacuated. This is an important point to discuss with the supplier, because different machines handle this problem more effectively than others.

Maintenance Consideration. In most shops, general day-to-day maintenance falls to the operator. This is a good policy, and, since the operator is familiar with the machine, he also knows when something is not performing correctly.

Each system has different maintenance requirements that are usually outlined in the service manual. Ask for information on the service intervals for different machines and compare them before selecting a system. This will indicate the amount of time per week used for keeping the laser in good running order and can affect the choice of machine.

Supplier Support and Service. Ask about the level of support that can be expected from the supplier. Even with a good training program, most companies need some assistance from the manufacturer of the equipment during the first month or two after installation.

Make sure that the company has technical support that can be accessed by telephone so that questions can be answered quickly. An operator cannot afford to wait if he has a processing question about a new material that has to be cut for a new customer.

Machine service is also important. A supplier's track record can be determined by speaking to existing customers.

Warranty. Read the warranty and understand what is and is not covered.

If the machine specifications call for a foundation or a special environment for the laser and a decision is made not to comply, how will the warranty be affected? Does the warranty cover travel expenses along with parts and labor?

Some companies do not put hour limitations on the warranty, while others place a 2,000-hour limit on the coverage. If a warranty is for one year or 2,000 hours and the machine will be run for two 10-hour shifts each day, the warranty will only cover the machine for 20 weeks.

The purchaser must ensure he knows what the laser supplier expects him to do to maintain the machine. If these questions are resolved before the machine purchase, there will not be any surprises for either the buyer or the seller.

It is difficult to quantify features of a machine such as beam delivery design and ease of use without seeing and testing each machine under consideration.

A visit to each potential supplier is important because nothing compares to watching the machine being set up and producing parts. Difficulties in loading or unloading material and setting up the machine will become apparent, especially if the demonstration closely resembles how the machine will be used in production.

Before going to a supplier, the purchaser should explain what he wants to see done and what material is to be cut. Watching a machine cut stainless steel without plastic coating is worthless if the purchaser plans to run only coated material.

If a supplier does not have samples of the right material, bring some along with prints and ask the manufacturer to make the part. If the manufacturer cannot or will not comply, consider a different laser system.

How to Justify a Laser Cutting System

After the costs of the laser system are determined, return on investment (ROI) calculations can be started. Rather than going through a complete justification, because each situation is different, this section highlights areas in which the laser can produce a payback.

Since the original equipment manufacturer (OEM) has different considerations than a job shop, each is addressed independently.

OEM. The OEM manufacturer is being forced to improve quality, deliver goods in less time, and reduce costs. Order quantities are shrinking, and product life cycles are being compressed. Inventory reduction or elimination is also directing companies to reevaluate existing production practices and move toward JIT manufacturing. Laser cutting machines can meet all of these requirements.

The CNC turret press was the first machine to offer flexibility and replace hard tooling and stamping. Typical setup time with a turret press is about 30 minutes on average. This is not a significant amount of time if a production run is large, but it is excessive if an order quantity of a few parts is required.

Many OEMs are using the laser for the shorter production runs with which setup is costly, while the turret press is being used for longer runs. The laser will not replace a turret press, but, when used in conjunction with a turret press, it allows a manufacturer to be more flexible and competitive.

Many OEMs are considering laser cutting systems to solve manufacturing problems, and a justification is built around cost savings or production improvements. Often, the laser will replace another process or be used with a turret press or other equipment.

This allows the laser to be justified in a quantitative way because savings in setup time or reduction in secondary operations are fairly easy to calculate.

The overall manufacturing process remains intact with this type of justification, and lot sizes are often slightly reduced or remain the same. An example of this type of justification is when the laser is used to produce parts in one operation that previously took three separate operations. The production improvements from reduced handling and WIP and faster turnaround are easy to document.

A few manufacturers are directing their efforts toward true JIT manufacturing and are using computer-integrated manufacturing (CIM) and equipment such as lasers to produce lot sizes of one or two parts efficiently.

The laser is an ideal tool for cutting an entire family of parts from a single sheet of material, which is a more efficient way to produce small lot sizes. This use of the laser necessitates a much broader view of the entire manufacturing process and usually requires a major revamping of all aspects of production.

This is the largest area for growth in the U.S. because competitive pressure will require companies to use the full advantage of equipment like laser cutting machines.

An area often overlooked during justification of the laser is the design department. Most small to medium-size OEMs design products around in-house capability or the ability of local subcontractors. In many instances, the addition of the laser allows products to be redesigned to reduce the number of components or to streamline assembly.

This benefit is difficult to quantify, but discussions with design engineering can often lead to cost savings with the laser cutting machine. The design engineering area is also involved in new products and creation of prototype parts. Laser cutting is commonly used for prototype or pre-production parts because no tooling is needed and changes can be made very quickly.

Job Shops. Contract manufacturers or job shops are also pressured to control costs and speed up deliveries. A job shop can also take advantage of the expanded capabilities the laser offers. Plastics, wood, and other material not processed in sheet metal job shops can now be cut with a laser.

The difficulty a job shop has in justifying a laser system is in making the financial commitment to purchase the laser.

Usually, a small company is confronted with the age-old dilemma, "I cannot pursue laser work until I have a machine, and I cannot buy the machine until I have the work to keep it busy." This is a constant problem, but one that has a solution. Every successful contract shop has a few large customers and many small ones.

Talk to current customers and explain the benefits a laser might have for them. The laser system will allow delivery times to be shortened, or work that is currently being sent to machine shops or wire EDM shops can be processed faster and at less cost with the laser.

Tooling charges can be eliminated, and shapes that could not be produced by punching can be generated with the laser. The laser is often a catalyst for turning small customers into large ones, especially when the contract shop can assist in product development and prototyping.

A company should set aside all the jobs that were not bid upon, or bid on and lost, so they can be reviewed with a laser cutting system in the picture. In many instances, a justification can be made on work available to a job shop that was not profitable with existing machinery.

A laser cutting machine can make current work more profitable and can help secure new customers because lead times can be reduced and tooling costs can be eliminated. The laser frees up the turret press to produce long runs, which it does more cost-efficiently than the 5- to 10-piece orders.

It is no accident that about 80 percent of all the laser cutting machines are in job shops. A contract manufacturer has to respond to a customer's needs for quality, delivery, and price. Often, the laser can answer these requirements.

Laser cutting machine sales have been increasing over the past few years for all the reasons stated previously.

Larger job shops have embraced laser cutting because the hourly rate generated by a laser can be twice as much as a punching machine. This is due in part to the newness of lasers and because there are still relatively few machines in the field.

Laser cutting machines have been around for more than 10 years, and the sheet metal industry is recognizing the advantages of this technology.

Common Misconceptions About Laser Cutting Systems

Some common questions and misconceptions about laser cutting machines should be addressed:

1. **Welding with cutting systems.** This is possible, but laser welding requires intimate contact between the parts to be joined and is usually used in areas in which the parts are heat-sensitive or in automated applications.

Laser welding is a nonadditive process and is difficult to do with laser cutting systems as they are configured. Cutting systems can be used for welding, but the limitations of the machine will make it difficult and not cost-effective.

2. **No setup time.** This is partially true because there are instances when almost no setup time is needed between jobs. Usually, setup between jobs takes five minutes, especially when the operator

has some experience with the equipment.

3. **Laser will replace turret punch machines.** Both machines offer different advantages, so it is not likely that the laser will replace a turret press. The laser advantages have been outlined previously. The turret press advantages become apparent when run quantities are large and the parts have many holes.

It comes down to using the right tool for the job, and, because of this, the laser will not replace a turret press, but complement it.

4. **A laser is as easy to use as a turret press.** Laser systems require more operator skill than turret presses. More variables exist in the setup of the laser, so the operator plays a critical role in the success of a laser installation. A good operator will be conscientious, attentive of details, and be willing to explore the capabilities of the equipment.

Conclusion

Laser cutting systems have evolved from a novelty seen at trade shows to an important tool that answers many of the needs of both OEMs and job shops.

Over the next decade, laser cutting machines will be as common as turret presses, primarily because of trends in manufacturing and market pressures. The proof of this can be found in Europe, Japan, and, more importantly, the more successful job shops in the U.S.

Creativity and a new approach to the manufacturing process is often the best way to generate a justification for laser equipment. The many advantages of laser systems allow a company to be more competitive and flexible.

There is no better time than now to explore the ways a laser system can enhance your capabilities and improve productivity and profitability.

Justifying CO$_2$ laser cutting: Reviewing machine configurations and machine purchasing criteria

Laser is an "exploding" technology for metal fabrication. The past several years have brought dramatic growth in implementation of this powerful tool in the industrialized world, especially Japan, Europe, and North America.

The most popular use of laser in metal fabrication is cutting, and the CO$_2$ laser continues to gain most of these installations.

In North America, the number of CO$_2$ installations is increasing by about 25 percent annually. Fabricators are cutting thicknesses of not only mild steel, but also stainless steel, aluminum, and alloys not practical or possible a few years ago.

Justification of this versatile tool can be based on a number of advantages, such as its increased flexibility, accuracy, or speed versus other processes such as computer numerically-controlled (CNC) punching or waterjet cutting.

However, the acquisition cost of these machines is high, so the selection of the proper combination of components for the application, necessary productivity, and cost versus performance is critical to a profitable purchase.

Resonator Design

The laser resonator is the machine component that generates the beam. Resonators are designed and constructed to deliver a consistent, intense spot of light.

The resonator works by applying electrical energy to excite the lasing medium — CO$_2$ and other gases — to stimulate an output of coherent light. The rate at which the electrical power and

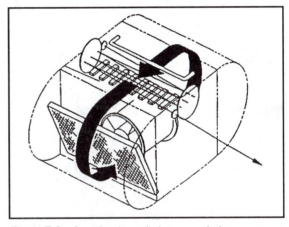

Figure 5-1. Crossflow laser design moves lasing gas across the electrodes.

the gases are consumed produces costs of operating the system. These rates vary by design.

Several different design concepts of the CO$_2$ laser are available. Crossflow or axial flow refer to the direction of lasing gas flow within the unit (see **Figure 5-1**). Electrodes to emit excitation energy can either be inside or outside the tube, and energy can be alternating current (AC), direct current (DC), or even radio frequency (RF) (see **Figure 5-2**).

Between design concepts, there can be a considerable difference (±20 percent) in resonator operating cost. Electrical efficiencies vary, so power consumption will vary.

Efficiency of gas flow varies, so the consumption of lasing gases varies (as much as 50 percent or more). Pulsing features such as Hyperpulse and Superpulse will operate at different costs than continuous wave (CW) cutting.

Therefore, resonator costs, both acquisition and operating, should be factored into the justification based on actual production requirements.

Inside the resonator, additional elements can create periodic costs. Internal electrodes will disintegrate during operation and form a deposit on internal mirrors that must be periodically cleaned. Mirrors will also require adjustments because of thermal stresses.

Replacement of these items is infrequent, but it produces cost in the labor expended and downtime required.

Machine Configuration

The size of sheet or plate to be cut, material thickness range, and requirements for blank or piece-art material handling and part tolerance are factors to evaluate in choosing the best machine configuration.*

In any laser machine configuration, the beam is focused by a lens within the head, located above the material. Also in the head is a means to direct pressurized cutting gas, such as oxygen or nitrogen, or water to the cut.

Prices of the cutting gases vary. Head, nozzle, and lens design also affect operating costs and may affect part quality. A difference in the diameter of the nozzle, assuming a constant pressure, will affect flowrate and, therefore, impact assist gas cost.

Based on a realistic survey of the materials to be cut, the part geometry, and lot sizes, the customer can select a CO_2 laser cutter for the application. The next step is to verify that it will do the job cost-effectively.

Purchasing the Machine

Following the steps discussed, a machine has been selected as the candidate for purchase.

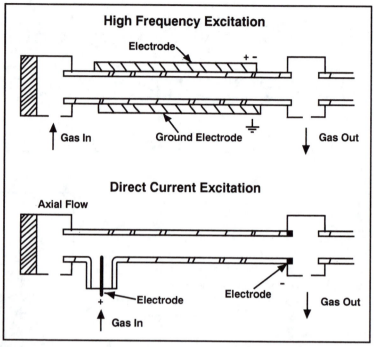

Figure 5-2. Different excitation means are possible in axial flow laser resonators.

For the purpose of determining the productivity of the candidate machine, a part has been selected. It will be assumed that the part is a 12-inch by ¼-inch square having ten 1-inch diameter internal holes.

It will then require 82 inches of contouring and 11 laser beam starts. The parts will be made out of 48-inch by 96-inch sheet at a cutting rate of 65 inches per minute (IPM).

To find the number of parts this machine will produce in a month, the time per part must first be determined by adding the time for beam starts plus contouring at 65 IPM (see **Figure 5-3**). This arrives at a total of 98 seconds.

Thirty-two parts come off each blank. A laser startup time of five minutes is also added. The pallet shift time is added, assuming a flying optics system. Next, the number of sheets or parts per eight-hour shift is found by dividing the time available in the shift, less a factor for consumable replacement, by the time per sheet of 3,196 sec-

* For specific information on these configurations, see "Selecting and justifying a laser cutting system," p. 24.

onds. This yields a daily production of 285 parts or 5,700 per 20-working-day month.

Based on an acquisition cost of $400,000, all costs can then be broken into a monthly schedule, which, for the purposes of the example, have been based on a plan with 10 percent down and a 60-month term. In **Figure 5-4**, the line item "machine cost" refers to the monthly cost of paying off the laser plus absorbing one sixtieth of the 10-percent down payment.

To this amount is added the monthly operating cost — a total of all variable costs such as gases, electrical power, labor, and consumables. As this total can vary depending on part mix, a representative part has been selected to determine this value.

This analysis shows that the cost per part — not considering material — is $2.48.

Knowing the cost per part, the profit level for the machine can be determined (see **Figure 5-5**).

The market will set the price for the parts based on a per-part or a per-hour basis. Allowing a $200-per-hour rate in the marketplace, the sales price per part as well as the margin can then be established.

Taking these steps, the profitability of a machine can be closely estimated. The purchase of a CO$_2$ laser cutter should be based on a thorough analysis of the unit's actual productivity and costs in making the purchaser's parts, sold at the margin available in the purchaser's market.

Productivity Analysis	
Time Per Part	$11 \times 2 + \frac{(82 \times 60)}{65} =$ 98 Seconds
Time Per Sheet	98 x 32 + 60 (Pallets) = 3,196 Seconds
Sheets/Parts	$\frac{8 \times 60 \times 60 - 5 \times 60 - 30}{3,196}$ 8.90 Sheets/285 Parts

Figure 5-3.

Part Cost/Price Analysis	
Machine Price	$399,000
Down Payment (10%)	$ 39,900
Balance Financed	$359,100
Monthly Payment @ 60-Month Financing	$ 7,897
1/60 Of Down Payment	$ 665
Machine Cost Per Month	$ 8,562
Monthly Operating Cost	$ 5,581
Number Parts Produced (Using the Example)	5,700
Cost Per Part	$ 2.48

Figure 5-4.

Profit Analysis	
Parts Per Hour	36
Sales Price Per Part	$ 5.61
Gross Income Per Hour	$ 202
Cost Per Hour	$ 88
Profit Per Hour	$ 114

Figure 5-5.

Five-axis CO_2 laser
machine tools
and laser machining

This article focuses on the selection and application of five-axis laser machine tools. The information is aimed specifically at multiaxis laser systems employing CO_2 lasers. Much of the material is generic in nature and may be applicable to other types of laser systems in the areas of machine motion mechanisms, controls, and optical system requirements. The information on processing should directly pertain to other systems as well.

The primary goal of this article is to provide insight into the problems commonly associated with large multiaxis laser systems and to present possible solutions to those problems. The intent is to provide adequate information to enable the end user to select, purchase, and apply five-axis laser systems successfully and to avoid many of the problems associated with the implementation of this equipment in the past.

Proper selection of the equipment, followed by correct application, is the key to success in the five-axis cutting world. The finest machine tool cannot do a task that it was not designed to accomplish.

Five-Axis Laser Systems

Machine Structures. Multiaxis laser systems are available in many configurations, each with merits and negative aspects. Machine structure, head design, controller design, optical system, and laser generator determine the end use for which the machine is best suited. So, the end user must fully understand the final application for the machine tool and make the final machine selection based on suitability of the system to accomplish the desired task.

Work envelope, system processing speed, acceleration, precision, and many other factors must be carefully examined as part of the evaluation process. Failure to identify the intended task and precision required may result in the purchase of equipment incapable of performance to the level required.

Regardless of the system type, accuracy and repeatability must be considered of prime importance for precision laser cutting. The drive train should be composed of drive components with no backlash, or provisions must be made available in controller software for backlash compensation.

The drive mechanism may be of the leadscrew type or the rack and pinion type. For the smaller systems, either drive system is suitable. For larger systems, however, a rack and pinion system may be more desirable because accuracy and acceleration may be difficult to maintain with large diameter, long-length leadscrews. Four common systems are round bar, linear motion bearing, knife-edge roller bearing, and air bearing. The round bar type may be unsuitable for large, high-accuracy machine tools.

The available machine configurations are shown in **Figure 6-1** and discussed in "Selecting and justifying a laser cutting system," on page 24 of this book. Two arm systems will be discussed here.

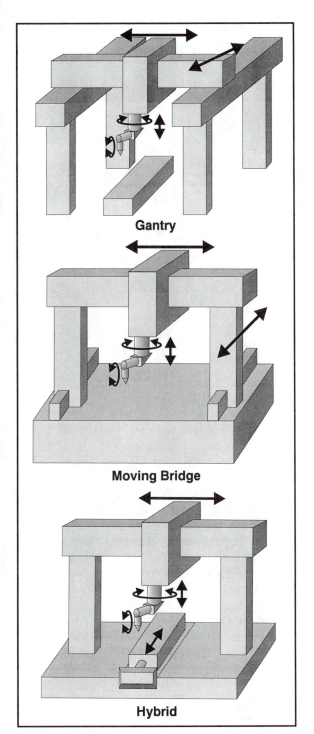

Gantry

Moving Bridge

Hybrid

Figure 6-1. Some available five-axis laser machine configurations are shown here.

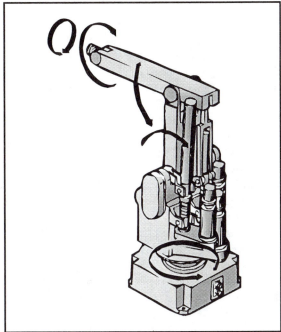

Figure 6-2. Articulated arm robots are the classic, familiar robot design.

Articulated arm robots are the classic, familiar robot design (see **Figure 6-2**). Most use a beam delivery system through the arm, although some of the early ones attempted to move the laser resonator on the arm. Beam delivery system alignment on some of these systems is difficult, and accuracy is a concern with these systems.

Several robots may be placed along side an automated line, allowing simple but effective pass-through production line capability. Part processing envelopes may be a limiting factor if only one unit is used. Reaching the opposite side of part may not be possible.

Cantilevered arm systems consist of a machine base and an overhanging arm (see **Figure 6-3**). The arm contains a carriage and the Z axis and rotary head mechanism. Good work envelope sizes are available with some units offering a rotating waist on the arm. This permits radially aligned work areas to be set up around the machine. In this way, one unit may serve several work stations.

Accuracy may be a problem on larger units because of the long moment arm of the cantilever itself. Some units tend to vibrate, which translates into loss of accuracy and "weave" introduced into the cut or weld path.

Controllers. Controllers may be divided into two distinct classes, with some hybrids blurring the distinction. The user must make certain that the control can handle the data stream supplied to the system. Computer-aided design/computer-aided manufacturing (CAD/CAM) output point stream may exceed the capability of the system to process data and move to positions.

Robotic controllers have not traditionally been considered user-friendly. They were designed for accomplishing a limited set of movement types and were normally programmed via self-teaching. These controls improved during the past decade and now represent a class of controllers which offer many computer numerical control (CNC) features.

Most robotic controls handle axis offsets (translation), multiplane path computation, and extended language commands. Some robotic controls may not be able to maintain the tool path accuracy needed for laser cutting and welding. Many were designed for control of traditional welding equipment, which requires less accuracy. Many of the hybrid controls closely resemble the robotic controls in the area of high-level language and multiplane interpolation and offer the CNC style of user interface.

CNC controllers are used on multaxis machining centers. These controls typically have

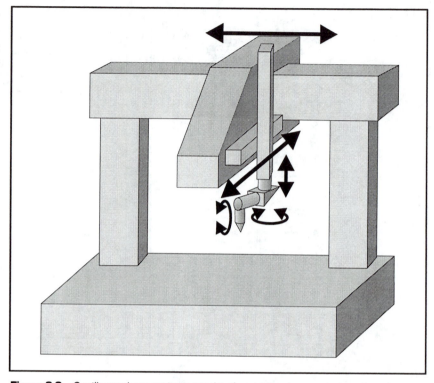

Figure 6-3. Cantilevered arm systems consist of a machine base and an overhanging arm.

good postprocessor support, easy-to-use interface, and standard language elements. Some units are not capable of full multiaxis in-space interpolation without the predefining of a working plane, and this limits the machine tool.

Additionally, some of the controls may not handle offset axes and tool centerpoint (TCP) positioning commands. This means they must be programmed at the individual joint level, which limits machine usability, especially in the area of self-teach programming. Some CNC controls do not allow teach mode programming.

Optical Chains. Beam delivery optical chains come in many configurations and may be the limiting factor in determining machine performance capability. The term "flying optics" is used here to describe all multiaxis laser systems using moving mirrors to direct the laser beam. Flying optics in the full gantry style are composed of at least four optics with one optic traveling with the main carriage, at least one directing the beam down into the Z column, and at least two mirrors in the head. In practice, however, most systems use more than four optics. Five or more optics may be considered typical. This excludes nonmoving optics. Some of the "constant tool tip position" head designs may use five optics in the head alone.

On large systems, a collimator is required to maintain correct beam diameter throughout the machine's work envelope. The two types of collimators are transmissive and reflective. Transmissive collimators resemble a "rifle scope" in appearance. They usually use two lenses for achieving up or down collimation. Reflective collimators use curved mirror sets to accomplish the up or down collimation required.

Cooling of head optics may be accomplished by water cooling or a combination of gas cooling and conduction. Water-cooled head optics are only required for welding applications or when laser output power exceeds two kilowatts. The inclusion of water-cooled optics usually forces the machine tool builder to limit head rotation.

Air-cooled head designs may employ 360-degree continuous rotation. The air-cooled versions use assist gas as the cooling agent for the bottom side of the focusing lens, and air is usually supplied to the top side of the focusing lens. This air flows past the lens, over the head optics, and usually into the Z axis column where it acts as a pressurizing agent. The head optics are cooled by a combination of this air flow and by the conduction of heat from the optic to the actual head structure. In effect, the head acts as a large heat sink. The amount of heat to be removed is relatively low.

Head Designs. Head designs vary dramatically from one system to another. The simplest design, the **offset head** (see **Figure 6-4**), employs two mirrors and one final focusing lens. This head actually has the TCP offset from the center of rotation of the first rotary and the Z column. The advantage of the offset design is simple alignment and a reduced number of optics. The disadvantage is that the controller must be able to handle offset calculations for five-axis in-space interpolation.

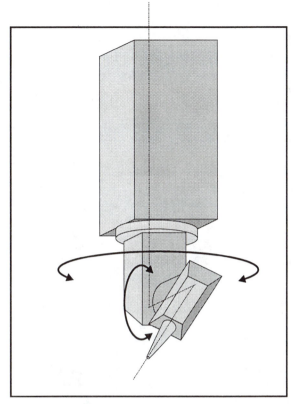

Figure 6-4. The offset head employs two mirrors and one final focusing lens.

Ideally, the head should offer 360 degrees continuous rotation of the first joint. This allows the user to program parts without periodically backing the head away from the work and "unwinding" the head. This unwinding results in slower and more complex part programming.

The more complex, **non-offset head** designs have four or more mirrors in the head, and the TCP is coaxial with the center of rotation of the first rotary axis (the Z axis column). The advantages of the non-offset design are that the controller does not need to have offset handling software, and performance may be better in the area of kinematic and dynamic behavior of the axes as small outside radii are contoured. Some types of head designs handle these moves totally within the head itself.

The disadvantages of non-offset head designs are that they usually contain more optics and are

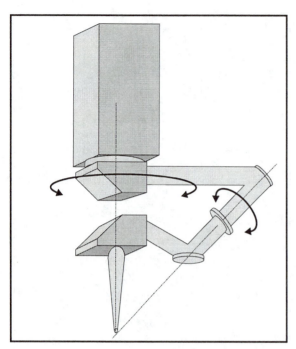

Figure 6-5. The constant tool centerpoint head is shown here.

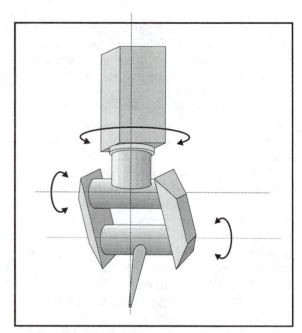

Figure 6-6. In the rotating Z-axis column design, the Z-axis column acts as the first rotary. Mechanical linkage extends downward through the Z column and into the head. This moves the B axis.

more difficult to align. They may be mechanically complex. Some of these head designs may be unusually large, making small-part processing difficult. **Figure 6-5** shows the constant TCP type.

In the **rotating Z-axis column** design, the Z-axis column acts as the first rotary (see **Figure 6-6**). Mechanical linkage extends downward through the Z column and into the head. This moves the B axis. These units are compact, but the design does not allow for inclusion of a workpiece sensor. The head may be mechanically complex and expensive to repair, and optics alignment may be difficult.

Moving Beam Systems

Work Envelope. Moving beam systems permit the design of relatively large work envelopes. The overhead gantry system offers the largest work envelope of any available machine configuration. Work envelopes range up to 40 feet long, 20 feet or more wide, and up to 10 feet tall, making these systems the largest available.

Freedom of Design. Freedom of design means

that the machine does not need to be designed around a limited fixed optical chain. This permits the system builder to design the machine to suit the task. This freedom has spawned the many different five-axis flying optics systems discussed in this article. Freedom of design allows the end user to select a system which best suits the intended processing needs.

Workpiece Fixturing. Fixed beam and rotary/tilt systems require the part to be moved in several directions to accomplish five-axis contouring. Moving beam systems usually do not require the part to be moved. In the worst case, parts may be moved in one linear axis. This simplifies part fixturing needs.

Load/Unload Systems. The overhead gantry and the moving beam gantry allow the part to remain stationary. This permits the integration of automatic loading and unloading devices. The overhead gantry offers the greatest possible number of choices for part and material handling options.

Integration with Factory Automation. Several of the moving beam systems lend themselves well to integration with factory automation schemes. The overhead gantry system offers the best possibilities, including a free work envelope floor allowing pass-through assembly lines and part conveying systems. The articulated arm robot lends itself well to line integration if more than one is installed to allow processing of both sides of the workpiece.

Potential Problems of Five-Axis Moving Beam Systems

Laser-to-Machine Tool Marriage. Extensive testing has been done using helium neon (HeNe) lasers and targets to determine what happens to the typical shop floor in the course of a day. Significant floor motion was detected as the building warmed up from exposure to sunlight. The building columns were moving as the roof and walls were heated and began to expand. The most significant areas of movement were around the walls of the structure and near building columns. This demonstrates the need for great care when installing machine tools.

An isolated, one-piece foundation is the only way to maintain the critical alignment of the laser to the machine tool. Some configurations of machines with short beam delivery paths will tolerate sitting on the shop floor but, in this case, "saw-cutting" a slab for the machine to isolate it from outside influences is recommended. The slab should be one continuous piece and should not extend across joints within the floor.

Optical Chain. Optical chains must be designed to withstand the acceleration and deceleration forces imposed on them by the movement of the machine tool. They must also be easy to align and service. Optics need periodic cleaning and/or replacement. After such operations, the optical chain usually must be realigned. The purpose of the alignment process is to direct the laser beam so that it travels parallel with and is centered within its designed travel path.

Additionally, if a HeNe laser is used, its beam must be aligned coaxially with that of the CO$_2$ laser. If a HeNe laser is used, transmissive optics should not be included in the beam delivery system because of the difficult alignment process between the two laser beams.

Optics should be mounted in front face reference mounts. This means that the front surface (the reflecting surface) of the optic is used to register the optic to its mount. When mounted in this manner, an optic may be removed for inspection or cleaning and replaced with little or no impact on the alignment of the optical chain.

Optics absorb a small percentage of the laser energy. This heat must be removed. The traditional method is to run water from the laser chiller through the optics. This solves the heat problem at the risk of causing a condensation problem because of the dew point of the air. Chiller water temperature setting is typically in the range from 55 to 80 degrees Fahrenheit, depending on the brand of laser being cooled. On warm, humid days, condensation will form on the optics, and wet optics will be destroyed if the laser beam is applied them.

The most common solution is to use a thermostatically-controlled cooling/heating loop for the optics to maintain the water at a preselected temperature. Another method is to use an air to water heat exchanger so that the optics coolant is supplied at room temperature or slightly higher. The heat load is very small, typically not much more than 10 percent of maximum power supplied by the laser. This is usually less expensive and eliminates the possibility that condensation will ever form on an optic because of the dew point.

Temperature Stability. Temperature stability is used in reference to both the machine tool and the workpiece. Large parts and machine tools are affected by changes in the ambient temperature.

Additionally, direct exposure to sunlight will cause expansion problems with the machine and the workpiece. The thermal expansion rate for the steel typically used in machine tools is about 0.0007 inch per foot per 10 degrees Fahrenheit temperature change. In some parts of the country, Work-In-Process (WIP) is stored outdoors.

In one recent case, the parts were approximately 25 feet long. The location was the midwestern U.S., so a temperature swing from 0 degrees to 100 degrees Fahrenheit (winter to direct sunlight exposure in summer) was examined. For this 100-degree range, 0.007 inch per linear foot growth/shrinkage is possible. For a 25-foot part, 1.75-inch part growth/shrinkage is possible. This range of temperatures is common and is often overlooked as the source of accuracy problems. Likewise, the machine tool itself will grow and shrink with changes in the ambient temperature. Great changes in temperature will cause misalignment of the laser optics and external beam delivery optics and will cause loss of machine accuracy.

In most cases, the system does not need to be installed in a temperature-controlled environment. However, the user should select an area that has a relatively stable temperature. Before processing, the workpiece should be allowed to reach the nominal ambient temperature at which the final inspection will be done.

The use of precision scale encoding devices for machine position information and the use of temperature compensation software may help to solve some of the problems. However, this type of problem is best solved by simply tightening the band of temperatures to which the workpiece and machine tool will be exposed.

Mechanical Limitations. Mechanical limitations include head size, laser power, machine repeatability, machine weight carrying capacity, and more. While every possible problem cannot be covered here, some of the most common ones are presented.

The basic design and form of the machine tool is the determining factor of the machine's limitations. The user should consider the following:

1. The resolution of the machine tool position feedback devices.

2. The smallest programmable increment for each axis.

3. The approximate increment of tool tip motion in linear units for each rotary axis move based on the smallest move increment, the resolution, and the repeatability. Axes with long joint lengths require better positioning capability. Make sure the machine is as accurate with its rotary axes as it is with the linear axes.

4. Availability of an anti-backlash system, accomplished via software or mechanically. For example, rack and pinion systems may use split gear sets with anti-backlash springs.

5. Actual head and nozzle size. Large units may not reach into areas of the workpiece where processing is needed.

6. Weight capacity of the machine tool. The user must know the maximum weight of part and fixture combined. This will determine which systems are suitable.

7. Machine strokes. Make certain the system will cover the necessary work envelope when the head is tilted to the 90-degree position.

8. Laser power available at the work (through the optics) that is adequate to perform the work. Allow a contingency of at least 5 percent power for safety.

9. A motion mechanism that delivers smooth "weave"-free tool trajectories. Surface finish will show striations and other blemishes introduced by machine-induced tool tip vibration and laser instability.

10. Adequate assist gas pressure and flow available at the cutting nozzle.

11. Full five-axis interpolation fast enough to keep up with the cutting speeds required.

Cutting Effluent and Debris. Laser processing effluent may include metal vapors and particles, organic compounds, acids, and other thermally-produced by-products. These materials may present operator health hazards, depending on actual exposure levels.

Some of these by-products may represent a threat to the machine's lifespan. When laser cut, some materials give off corrosive by-products

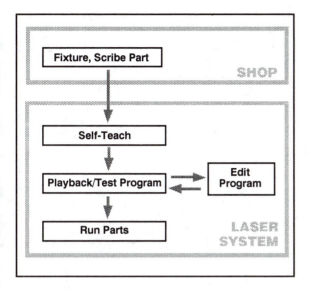

Figure 6-7. This diagram shows the self-teaching programming method.

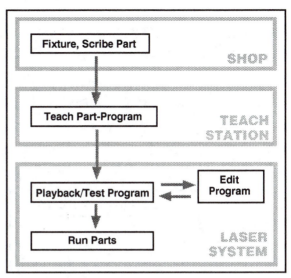

Figure 6-8. The off-line teach method uses a second machine, either detached or integrated, for teach programs.

which may attack various machine components.The inclusion of an effluent control system is essential. The proper system must be determined based upon the type of materials to be processed.

Workpiece Variations. The actual forming processes used for the creation of three-dimensionally (3-D) shaped parts usually introduces variations in the parts from one to the next. These variances are the result of wear in the dies and other process changes. In some instances, the part may not even fit onto the fixture properly. Some fixtures may incorporate suction devices and/or clamping devices for pulling the part into the desired shape.

Parts which are slightly out of tolerance may be processed by a machine using a workpiece sensor. Be aware that overall accuracy will suffer because the part is not in its true shape, which is not the fault of the machine.

Programming. A multiaxis laser system may be programmed in five different ways:

1. **Self-teach** (see **Figure 6-7**). This term is commonly used to describe the process of leading the machine tool through a series of moves and recording these moves in the controller's memory. The moves may be played back as a part pro-

gram. This method is used most commonly for accomplishing five-axis programming.

The part must be scribed with a line which represents the desired cut path. The operator then uses either a stylus or a visible laser (usually HeNe) as a guide for jogging the machine and recording the movement instruction. This method allows perfect clearance checking of the head while the part is being programmed because the actual cutting head is used as the programming tool.

The primary disadvantage of this method is that the system must be taken out of production during the programming operation. Programming may take up to 10 hours or more depending on the complexity of the part.

2. **Off-line teach** (see **Figure 6-8**). This method uses a second machine, either detached or integrated, for teach programs. The laser system may be processing parts while another operator is teaching programs. The unit usually includes a head which closely approximates the encumbrance of the actual cutting head. This allows good clearance checking while programming.

The advantages of this method are that production time on the laser unit is not wasted, and

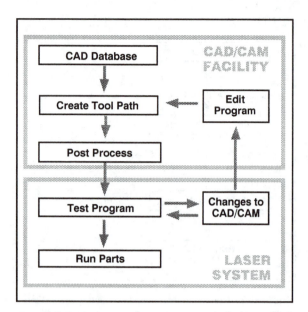

Figure 6-9. The CAD/CAM system programming method is shown here.

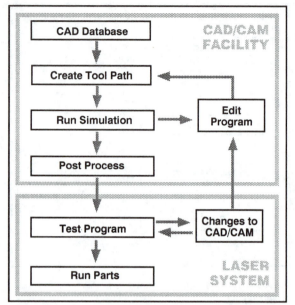

Figure 6-10. Graphics workstation platforms allow the user to build accurate models of the machine tool, fixtures, and parts.

program development time is usually shorter because the teaching machines are usually nonpowered. The axes may be quickly positioned by dragging them into position manually and recording the appropriate movement instruction. The stand-alone units may be placed in a quiet room away from shop activity and noise, which offers a better atmosphere for programming.

3. **CAD/CAM systems** (see **Figure 6-9**). Implementation of CAD/CAM systems for programming five-axis systems has been slow. Most of the early 3-D CAD/CAM systems could not generate five simultaneous motion commands. This situation was further hampered because of the high cost of hardware platforms, but this cost has come down in the past five years.

The main disadvantage of CAD/CAM-generated programs is that some have been directly responsible for machine "crashes." The two factors contributing to this are lack of meaningful collision checking between the head (or other machine members) and the workpiece (or fixture) in the CAD/CAM system and poor operator program path verification during dry-run. Furthermore, customers have discovered that programs generated

from databases usually do not match the actual parts being produced in the field.

4. **Simulator packages** (see **Figure 6-10**). Several high-end graphics workstation platforms are used for true machine modeling and simulation. These systems allow the user to build accurate models of the machine tool, fixtures, and parts.

They accept CAD data for surface and tool path generation. The user then walks the system through a simulation of the machine processing the part. The user may adjust program path and head angles, add instructions, and finally post the data into the machine tool's native language.

Some of these systems can feed program instructions to the machine tool in a true direct numerical control (DNC) format, in which the machine tool is controlled from a remote computer. Some simulator systems are capable of true DNC operation, but they may be expensive.

5. **Line follower systems** (see **Figure 6-11**). Line followers follow a line the user applies to the work part. The line usually consists of a tape that must be manually applied to the part along the desired tool path. The application of the tape can

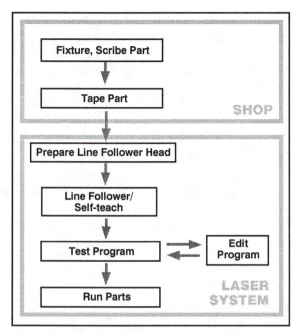

Figure 6-11. Line follower systems follow a line the user applies to the work part.

be time-consuming and lead to accuracy problems, but these systems can work for some applications.

The machine uses an optical feedback device for gathering cutting path data. The machine usually weaves back and forth, finding the boundary of the tape and looking for the contrast between the dark tape and the shiny workpiece.

The disadvantages of these systems are that the tape must be manually applied and the machine is used for the actual programming. Some systems have been developed which will follow a line in real time and laser trim the path. These systems are often expensive and require large amounts of computer hardware to accomplish the task.

Safety. NCDRH Requirements. The National Center for Devices and Radiological Health (NCDRH) is the primary government agency controlling laser system safety. Laser safety classification is based on the level of possible exposure to laser radiation for the operator. The classes range from I to IV. Class IV is the category most laser machine tools fall into. This means that the operator could be exposed to direct or scattered laser radiation. Class I systems are designed to contain the laser system completely, making it difficult or impossible for the operator to be exposed to laser radiation.

Moving Part Access. An operator might be exposed to moving parts of the machine tool if safety devices are defeated or rendered inoperative. Care should be taken to ensure that proper safety interlocks and devices are left intact and are fully functional.

Effluent. Cutting effluent may contain material that is potentially harmful to humans. The effective control and containment of this effluent must be considered when installing the machine. It is usually easier to install fume removal and control systems during the machine tool installation than to add them later.

Advice for Using Flying Optics

Focal Point Control. It is extremely important that the correct nozzle stand-off distance be maintained. Some type of workpiece sensor is mandatory for processing sheet metal parts. The sensor compensates for slight variations from one part to the next and for minor part fit-up problems with the fixture. Noncontact sensors are available in capacitive, inductive, and laser diode styles.

Assist Gas Delivery System. To Clean Cut™ with a laser, relatively high flow rates (depending on orifice size) at delivery gas pressures of up to 300 pounds for square inch (PSI) must be available at the cutting nozzle. Flow rates and delivery requirements are application specific and will not be discussed here.

Laser Cutting Parameter Documentation and Quality Control. To produce parts to tight tolerances and with good cut edge quality, a mechanism for laser beam analysis is required. A method for determining power loss through the optical chain, laser mode, and laser resonator performance must also be included. Some of the available devices are spinning wire laser beam profile instruments, precision power meters, chart recorders, and oscilloscopes. Laser power feedback devices may also be used to control laser output power in real time.

Clean Cut™ is a trademark of U.S. Amada, Ltd.

With these and other instruments, laser characteristics and optical chain condition can be monitored for the purpose of process documentation and preventive maintenance monitoring.

Clean Cutting on Five-Axis Machines. To produce clean, high-speed cuts, the user must verify gas pressure, nozzle orifice diameter, nozzle configuration, assist gas type, focal point, laser parameters, optics condition and alignment, and many other parameters. Additionally, the machine tool must include a workpiece sensor, provide smooth high-speed contouring tool tip motion, and have a good machine tool-to-laser interface.

Clean cutting is a combination of machine capability, laser capability, and operator setup. Today's machine tools can produce good-quality cuts as long as the end user properly establishes parameters for the process. Parameter development and recording is an important part of the laser fabricating process.

Alignment. To use flying optics for precision cutting, the external optical chain must be precisely aligned. An automatic beam alignment system is recommended. If a manual alignment system is used, the adjustment procedure must be well-defined and all necessary adjustment controls must be accessible to promote the regular alignment process.

Potential Markets for Five-Axis Laser Processing

This section does not discuss actual applications, but instead suggests possible areas in which the technology may be applied.

Aerospace. Common applications include trimming of stretch-formed aluminum parts and drop-hammer or press-formed aluminum and titanium parts. These may be skin panels or flight hardware. The Hastalloy® family and other exotic metals may be processed cleanly.

Automotive. The automotive industry is one of the largest users of this technology. Five-axis laser cutting can be used for developing prototype parts, manufacturing limited-run replacement parts, and customizing vehicles in the line.

Other. Other areas may include the heavy truck industry for the production line trimming of cab parts, frame assemblies, and hardware.

In general, most 3-D shaped parts are candidates for laser processing. The elimination of hard tooling, the subsequent reduction in delivery time, the reduction in labor requirements, and improved accuracy and quality make laser processing worth serious investigation.

Five-Axis Laser Case Study

This case study focuses on a fabricating company which serves the automotive, aerospace, farm implement, and recreational industries and helps them identify and solve potential prior to production.

This prototype manufacturer has invested in computer-integrated manufacturing (CIM) facilities and equipment. Included in the CIM inventory is a fully-equipped CAD/CAM facility, CNC milling machines, computer-operated presses and other metal forming equipment, coordinate measuring machine (CMM) inspection equipment, and five-axis laser metal cutting centers. A common math database is used at each stage of the manufacturing process to ensure that the finished parts will meet the specified blueprint tolerances.

The laser centers, with six-axis gantry robots, are used as replacements to the traditional hand finishing of prototype parts. Operating from computer-generated programs, laser cutting is an improvement over the time-consuming manual methods used to incorporate holes and slots and to perform final trim operations. Lasers perform all of these functions with speed, repeatability, and accuracy, which allows the company to process increased quantities of parts in a shorter period of time.

In addition to part-trimming operations, the lasers support the company's stamping operations by custom cutting sheet stock blanks for the press department. The speed, accuracy, and repeatability of laser cutting save labor time as compared to manual blank preparation. Intermediate trim operations are also performed on stampings before they are scheduled through restrike and flanging die operations.

The Hastalloy® trademark is owned by Haynes Corporation.

Replacing other fabricating operations with laser cutting: Applications ranging from stamping to tube cutting

The ability for fabricators to machine intricate patterns in a range of materials with short turnaround and low tooling costs has made laser cutting an important fabricating tool.

This article discusses common applications of laser cutting.

Low-Volume Stamping

Low-volume stampings produced in short-run production or in prototyping during the design phase are good candidates for laser cutting. Conventional means for producing these, such as temporary dies, can be both time-consuming and expensive.

Costs for temporary progressive dies can be in the tens of thousands of dollars. Delivery time for these is typically several months.

Furthermore, design changes, which are often necessary in the prototype stage, are often not possible with temporary dies.

These problems can be eased by a computer-controlled laser cutting system. The tooling consists of a numerical control (NC) part program that describes part geometry and all process conditions.

Time and cost to generate the "tooling" is considerably less than that required to fabricate or configure conventional tooling, particularly when the laser cutting system is interfaced to computer-aided design (CAD) equipment. Furthermore, the "tooling" can be quickly modified for optimizing part design.

With laser cutting, setup is minimal and can be accomplished in a short time. Part programs are loaded into the computer numerical control (CNC) through a variety of means, including distributed numerical control (DNC) interface and floppy disk.

Since no mechanical forces are applied to the workpiece, fixturing is simplified. For flat stock cutting, a universal fixture (cutter box) can be used for all applications.

Since the laser beam is a nonconsumable cutting "tool," there is no tooling, tooling preparation, or tooling maintenance with laser cutting. Rust, dirt, and oils are vaporized by the laser, so no cleaning or other preparation of the part material is required.

Piercing/Trimming 3-D Parts

Lasers offer many of the same advantages in machining formed metal and nonmetal parts as described for low-volume stampings. Applications include:

1. Trimming drawn, hydroformed, and spun metal parts.

2. Trimming thermoformed and molded composites.

3. Hole drilling and piercing.

4. Machining mounting holes and cutouts.

In low-volume and prototype manufacturing, formed parts are often trimmed with hand tools (such as metal snippers or hand routers) or manually-operated milling machines. Despite their low productivity, labor-intensive methods are often more economical for short runs and low volumes than hard tooling (trim die) methods.

The high cutting rates and precision associated with laser cutting make it an alternative to conventional machining and routing processes. For example, in replacing conventional machining, laser cutting has increased throughput in trimming a deep-drawn gas turbine engine component from 18 pieces per day to 18 pieces in 30 minutes.

Laser cutting can also offer productivity improvements over die trimming and piercing operations.

With laser cutting, setup involves mounting the minimal amount of fixturing required to locate the workpiece relative to the cutting head. Once this is done, the NC program describing the machining parameters (laser process conditions) and sequence (motion path) is loaded into the CNC.

This is accomplished in minutes, in contrast to hours for setup of hard tooling. Lower trimming rates of laser cutting compared to hard trim dies are more than offset by the almost negligible tooling setup time.

Tube Cutting

For a major aircraft manufacturer, laser cutting has replaced hand methods for cutting intersecting thin-wall aluminum and stainless steel tubing used in aircraft ducting. With the hand methods, one assembly was produced every 1½ hours. With laser cutting, the rate has been increased to one assembly every minute.

For another, laser cutting has replaced carbide cutting tool machining for drilling varying diameter holes in a high-strength composite.

The advantage is that laser cutting has a negligible effect on the composite matrix surrounding the hole. Conventional cutting methods reduce the composite strength by tearing the fibers from the matrix.

Also, because it defocuses as it exits the cut, the laser beam does not affect the adjacent side of the tubing.

The benefits of lasers for tube cutting applications illustrated in these and other applications include:

1. Flexibility in the type and shape of the cut. Laser cutting is used for producing a range of shapes, including holes from 0.006-inch diameter, slots, and cutouts for intersecting tubing.

2. Flexibility in type of material. Laser cutting is applied to a range of materials, including metals, plastics, and composites. It is also used for cutting a variety of tubing shapes and cross sections.

3. Elimination of distortion or deformation of the tubing material, since there is no mechanical force associated with a tool. This results in dimensional control (accuracy and repeatability). Also, additional processing to reshape distorted tubing is eliminated.

4. Higher throughput than with hand and conventional machining methods because of high cutting rates.

5. Precision accuracy in cut lengths better than ±0.005 inch. Accuracy of feature dimensions is ±0.002 inch.

The growing number of successful installations of multiaxis laser cutting and welding systems is demonstrating the ability of these systems to provide meaningful solutions to real-world laser cutting, drilling, and welding problems.

Of particular importance to manufacturers are the benefits of reduced tooling expense, flexible and quick setup for economical small lot manufacturing, and fast turnaround on prototype and production parts necessary to reduce the time to develop and bring new products to market.

Why isn't there a laser in every sheet metal job shop?: Why European and Japanese shops buy more laser cutters than the U.S.

For more than a decade, lasers have been referred to as a "wonder tool" which would revolutionize manufacturing. This idea has held sway, particularly in the precision sheet metal industry. Yet, in spite of this, their actual numbers in American industry remain surprisingly small.

In the U.S., in 1989, there were approximately 6,000 precision sheet metal job shops. Only about 200 of them (3 percent) had laser cutters. Certainly, some shops used an outside source for sheet metal cutting, but the fact remains that only a relatively small number of these shops actually owned a laser cutting machine.

Since lasers do a great job of cutting sheet metal, and shops with laser cutters have a competitive edge that they can exploit, what would explain this low percentage?

It is certainly not that lasers are inherently lacking in their capability to cut sheet metal. For almost 10 years, both European and Japanese manufacturers have been using laser cutting machines as a production tool on a routine basis.

Japan — which has an economy about half the size of the U.S.'s — has more than five times as many laser cutting machines as the U.S. In Europe, Germany alone is annually purchasing more laser cutting machines than are sold in the U.S. Why is this?

Manufacturing Methodology

A major factor is variation in manufacturing methods used in different parts of the world. Whereas the Just-In-Time (JIT) method of manufacturing has been in effect in Japan — and to some extent in Europe — for many years, it is just beginning to come into vogue in the U.S.

The JIT method mandates short production runs, and since lasers do not require much setup, they are great manufacturing tools for this type of production.

As the JIT manufacturing concept becomes more prevalent in the precision sheet metal industry, laser cutting machines will increase in number.

Partnering

Another trend which should accelerate the acceptance of laser cutting systems is the concept of "partnering." This is an arrangement between a manufacturer and his suppliers whereby they collaborate closely to minimize overall production costs.

Like JIT, this approach has been accomplished outside the U.S. for some time, while only a few forward-thinking companies in the U.S. have embraced this concept.

In this country, an adversarial relationship is still primarily retained between subsuppliers and manufacturers. Instead of inviting suppliers in at the beginning of the design process, when they can help the most, the manufacturer goes to them for bids only after the parts are designed.

The purchasing department then tries to achieve the absolute minimum price. This is a shortsighted approach which sacrifices long-term cost considerations.

In contrast, partnering places a premium on the supplier's ability to work with the manufacturer at every stage, from concept to first prototype and through all of the product revisions. The laser cutter's flexibility makes it a suitable choice for this type of working relationship.

As the partnering concept becomes more prevalent in the U.S., the use of laser equipment can be expected to rise in turn.

Advanced Technology

Although laser cutters are accepted as run-of-the-mill machine tools in Europe and Japan, they are still considered "advanced technology" in the U.S.

It is possible to visit job shops in Europe and Japan that have both laser cutting machines and a dirt floor, yet it seems that only the more forward-looking companies in this country are willing to consider laser cutters as a potential purchase. However, this is changing as the installed base of laser cutting machines continues to increase.

In addition, the competition between laser equipment manufacturers is helping to increase the awareness of laser cutting machines in the precision sheet metal market. This is occurring as the various manufacturers participate extensively in trade shows and technical seminars, while advertising their products widely.

For these reasons, laser cutting machines will soon no longer be considered exotic "advanced technology," and the hesitation felt by many potential users will evaporate.

Cost Factors

There is a widely-held belief that laser cutting machines are "expensive" to buy and use. Certainly a two-axis laser cutting machine cannot be considered a "casual" purchase, which concerns companies looking at a monthly payment of several thousand dollars.

While these are significant costs, they are often in line with those expected for the purchase of a similarly-sized computer numerically-controlled (CNC) turret press or CNC chip cutting machine when perishable tooling is taken into account. Also, the hourly revenue from a laser cutter can be several hundred dollars more than that from a turret press or similar chip cutting machine, depending on the application and location. There are also usually fewer laser cutters in an area, which means less competition for that revenue.

Unrealistic Expectations

Lasers are like other machine tools in that users get out of them what they put into them. They are not magic. They cannot work by themselves. They must be used in conjunction with a trained programmer/operator who understands how to get the best out of them.

Unfortunately, lasers are sometimes presented as machines that, with a few simple keystrokes, will calculate all of the cutting parameters, set themselves for the best/fastest cutting speeds available, and produce parts without further thought or concern. This is simply not true.

As with other machine tools, the person operating the machine has a significant degree of responsibility for the success or failure of that machine to work properly and to produce a profit for the shop owner.

If the wrong person is assigned to program and run the machine, it will not matter how good the machine is or how smart the CNC system is; the machine will not produce to its potential.

The unrealistic expectations of past years are now giving way to the realization that lasers are powerful machine tools that simply need the correct amount of attention and support to produce a quality product.

The one factor that remains constant is that most successful users of laser equipment, in the U.S. and elsewhere, are good businesspeople who would be successful even without lasers. This is because they recognize both the capabilities and the limitations of their equipment and do the best they can with this knowledge.

Laser cutting special materials and shapes: Defining unsuitable areas for laser processing

Some believe that anything at all can be cut with a laser processing machine.

It is true that laser processing machines can cut materials regardless of how hard or soft they are. However, if the cut material is not acceptable for use as a product, or if another method is cheaper, then it is meaningless to use laser processing. It is important to know the materials and methods for which laser processing is not suitable.

Difficult Materials

Highly Reflective Materials. Materials such as gold, silver, aluminum, molybdenum, etc., reflect almost all energy at the wavelength produced by a CO_2 laser (10.6μm) (34.78μft), as shown in **Figure 7-1**.

Therefore, if a laser processing machine generates 1kW of unfocused energy, for example, less than 50kW of the focused beam is actually absorbed by the material, so that the material is extremely difficult to cut. However, energy absorption increases when these materials melt, so that it is possible to cut thin sheets of these materials.

Materials with High Melting-Point Oxides. Molten oxides readily cool and adhere to the bottom surface as dross when materials having oxides with a higher melting point than the melting point of the parent metal itself, such as aluminum and stainless steel, are cut (see **Figure 7-2**).

Materials with High Viscosity. Molten aluminum, stainless steel, titanium, etc., have high viscosity when melted; thus molten metal is prone to adhere as dross. To avoid this, assist gas pressure should be increased to remove molten metal from the cut area more quickly.

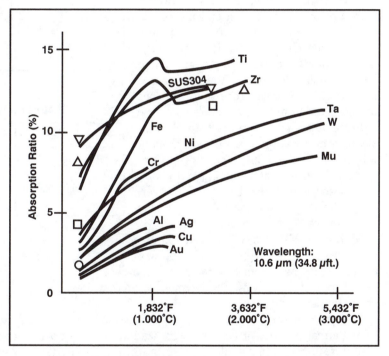

Figure 7-1. The absorption ratio of materials is shown here.

Materials with High Thermal Conductivity. As shown in **Figure 7-3**, materials with high thermal conductivity, such as aluminum and copper, disperse absorbed heat quickly. For this reason, higher power is required to cut these materials than mild steel, for example.

Flammable Metallic Materials. It is difficult to cut thick sheets of materials such as titanium which self-burn when heated in oxygen. Inert gas at higher pressures must be used as the assist gas.

Materials Highly Transparent to CO_2 Laser Light. Almost all light from a CO_2 laser passes straight through gallium arsenide and ZnSe, so that the light energy is not converted to heat energy, and cutting is impossible. Because of this, the lenses used in CO_2 gas laser processing machines are produced from these materials.

Materials with High Melting Points. Because of the very high melting points of tungsten, molybdenum, etc., they do not instantaneously reach melting point and are consequently difficult to cut. However, thin sheets of these materials can usually be cut effectively (see **Figure 7-4**).

Materials with High Thermal Expansion. Materials with high thermal expansion, such as glass, can crack from thermal stresses on cooling. Types of glass with low thermal expansion characteristics can be cut.

Organic Materials. Because laser processing is a thermal process, it causes carbonization or discoloration of almost all organic materials. Extreme caution is advised when cutting organics because of the poisonous gases produced by many organic materials.

Composite Materials or Materials with Protective Covering. The thermal characteristics differ for each material in the composite. Therefore, if the laser is adjusted to cut a material with high thermal strength, too much heat might be input to materials with lower thermal strengths, causing pronounced thermal effects and cutting difficulty.

Materials with High Melting-Point Oxides

Property \ Material	Aluminum	Stainless Steel	Mild Steel
Melting Point °F (°C)	1,220 (660)	2,588 (1,420)	2,678 (1,470)
Melting Point of Oxide °F (°C)	3,718.4 (2,048) (Al_2O_3)	4,127 (2,275) (Cr_2O_3)	2,516 (1,380) (FeO)

Figure 7-2.

Materials with High Thermal Conductivity

	Aluminum	Copper	Mild Steel
Thermal Conductivity ($W^{.m.1}.K^{.1}$)	238	403	48

Figure 7-3.

Materials with High Melting Points

	Tungsten	Molybdenum
Melting Point °F (°C)	6,128.6° F (3,387° C)	4,730° F (2,610° C)
Boiling Point °F (°C)	10,700.6° F (5,927° C)	8,679.2° F (4,804° C)

Figure 7-4.

For example:

Metal + polyethylene or polypropylene to protect the surface = Carbonization, melting

Materials with protective coatings with elastic properties can cause a balloon effect when piercing takes place. New techniques, such as precutting the protective covering first and then repiercing the material, are helping to overcome this problem.

Laminated Material. When laminated materials are cut or if material is stacked, the assist gas escapes sideways along the cut layers so that a quality cut cannot be obtained.

Other Dangerous Materials. Carefully process the dust produced by cutting asbestos, as this is carcinogenic. Beware of reflected laser light when cutting or marking a highly-reflective mate-

Cutting Aluminum Alloy				
Material	**Thickness**	**Wattage**	**Feed Rate**	**Assist Gas Type and Pressure**
A5025	.078 in. (2.0t)	1 kW	F1000 (39 IPM)	Nitrogen 8Kg (120 PSI)
A5025	.118 in. (3.0t)	1.5 kW	F800 (32 IPM)	Nitrogen 8Kg (120 PSI)
No. 1000 = pure aluminum No. 2000 = copper based (2017 = duralumins) No. 3000 = manganese based		No. 4000 = silicon based No. 5000 = magnesium based No. 6000 = magnesium and silicon based No. 7000 = zinc and magnesium based		

Figure 7-5.

Cutting Titanium			
Thickness	**Wattage**	**Feed Rate**	**Assist Gas Type and Pressure**
.078 in. (3.0t)	1.0 kW	F1000 (39 IPM)	Argon 7Kg (105 PSI)
.195 in. (5.0t)	1.5 kW	F700 (26 IPM)	Argon 7Kg (105 PSI)
Note: A pressure-resistant lens is required when cutting aluminum or titanium. Also, it is convenient to have a third assist gas port if these materials are cut a high proportion of the time.			

Figure 7-6.

rial. Take care to shield from the bright light which is produced when quartz glass or titanium is cut. Suitable equipment is required to process the gases and smoke particulate produced when organic materials are cut.

Materials That Must Never be Cut. Vinyl chloride and vinyl chloride coatings must never be cut by laser as the chlorine gas produced is extremely poisonous to humans and causes rapid corrosion of the machine. Also, take care with vulcanized rubber and ABS resin.

Cutting Aluminum Alloy

Higher power is required to cut aluminum because of its high reflectivity to CO_2 laser light and its high thermal conductivity. It also suffers dross adhesion because the melting point of its oxide is higher than that of the parent metal (1,220 degrees Fahrenheit or 660 degrees Celsius for aluminum, 3,718.4 degrees Fahrenheit or 2,048 degrees Celsius for aluminum oxide) and because of the high viscosity of the molten material.

Aluminum alloys are classified according to the additives they contain (see **Figure 7-5**). With the exception of the No. 1000 and No. 2000, all these alloys can be cut if the output power exceeds 1kW.

Cutting Titanium

Titanium burns when heated in contact with oxygen, so that cutting has to be carried out with a shield gas in place of an assist gas (oxygen). Also, argon must be used as the shield gas as titanium reacts with nitrogen at 1,472 degrees Fahrenheit (800 degrees Celsius) to produce titanium nitride. A high shield gas pressure is also required because of the high viscosity of molten titanium (see **Figure 7-6**). These factors make the cost of cutting titanium higher than for other materials.

Box Shapes

It is possible to cut holes in the top surface of box-shaped workpieces after bending or in rectangular section pipe, but the height and length are limited by the machine stroke length. In some machine styles, the height can be increased to the

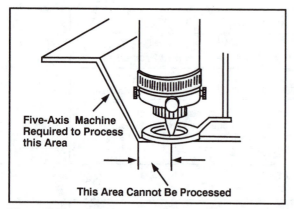

Figure 7-7. A five-axis machine is required to process a hole on an incline.

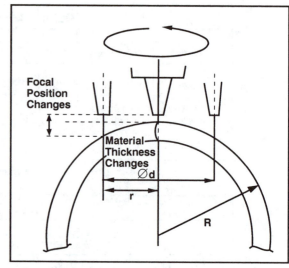

Figure 7-8. Processing of round pipes is shown here.

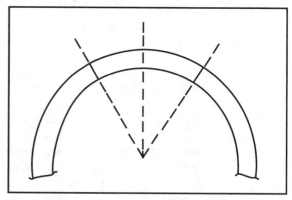

Figure 7-9. The radius limitation does not apply if processing is done as shown here.

Z-axis stroke + 3.15 inch (80 millimeters), removing the support spikes, to make a jig or fixture.

Because of interference between the workpiece and the torch, some areas of a workpiece with a stepped surface cannot be processed. These unprocessed areas (dead zones) depend on the height and angle of the steps.

Usually, a three-axis laser is only capable of processing horizontal areas. There can be a 10 to 15 degree cut in some parts. A five-axis machine (three-dimensional machine) is required to process a hole on the incline (see **Figure 7-7**).

Round Pipes

Circular commands in the X and Y planes must be given to cut a hole in a round pipe to pass a round bar through the pipe (see **Figure 7-8**). However, the radius is limited by the relationship $R>5r^2$ because of the changing gap between the nozzle and workpiece (focal point) and the changing thickness of the material to be cut.

This limitation does not apply if the processing is carried out as shown in **Figure 7-9**. However, this processing requires an additional axis and cylinder interpolation functions.

Nonoxidation Cutting

In normal laser cutting operations, an intense reaction is caused by driving oxygen against the material which has been heated to a high temperature by the laser. The heat produced by this oxi-

dation reaction causes the continuous melting and cutting of the material. This results in an oxide layer on the cutting surface which must be removed if seam welding, electroplating, electrostatic painting, or electrode-position painting is to be carried out after the material is cut.

When stainless steel is cut, the resulting discoloration must be removed by subsequently washing with acid if the finished appearance of the product is important. In some cases, the need for this type of postprocessing can be eliminated by carrying out nonoxidizing cutting.

Nonoxidation cutting refers to the technique of replacing the oxygen assist gas with an inert shield gas of nitrogen or argon so that cutting the metal is carried out only by the energy of the laser, and assisted by gas pressures four to five times higher than when using oxygen. Operating costs are therefore higher.

This method completely eliminates the oxide layer and discoloration, but its use is realistically limited to stainless steel sheet up to 0.090 inch (2.28 millimeters) thick. Thicker materials can be processed, but material thickness variations or waviness of the material can cause sporadic, much harder, parent material dross to adhere to the bottom of the cut. This is commonly due to focus point variation when cutting material with these characteristics at higher speeds.

Staying competitive using five-axis laser clean cutting: How to improve the quality of three-dimensional parts

The majority of leading high-tech manufacturing companies now know that to stay competitive in today's challenging business environment, they need to use state-of-the-art manufacturing equipment such as lasers, which vary in capabilities and sophistication. Lasers — from simple two-axis flatcutters to five-axis robotic laser systems — are now regarded as today's technology, rather than that of the 21st century.

Whether companies choose to purchase their own equipment or use a laser job shop, laser cutting has passed the experimental stage and demonstrated practical benefits to the aerospace and other manufacturing industries involved in the fabrication of metal and composite parts.

Just-In-Time (JIT) manufacturing concepts can be enhanced through the use of laser cutting. In most industries, producing quality parts on a timely basis is a "must." Compared to the complex hard tooling that must be generated for processes such as machining and stamping, lasers have the advantage of relatively fast programming and flexibility. The ability to program, tool, and process quickly makes laser cutting an optimal choice for meeting JIT requirements.

To understand better how and when to use lasers, laser clean cutting, and five-axis lasers with clean cutting capabilities in manufacturing, it is necessary to review types of lasers used for various applications and the Clean Cut™ technique.

Industrial Laser Overview

The most common types of lasers for manufacturing include the Nd:YAG, a solid-state laser, and CO_2, a gas-type laser. Both of these lasers can perform tasks such as cutting, drilling, welding, scribing, and selective heat treating.

Lasers are typically configured with computer numerical control (CNC) capability, using either a moving table or moving optics that can interface with off-line computer-aided design/computer-aided manufacturing (CAD/CAM) equipment.

CO_2 lasers are widely used because they can cut at high speeds in most materials. CO_2 lasers can cut, drill, and scribe metal and composites, as well as weld and selectively heat treat all types of metals. Metals compatible with CO_2 laser processing include steels, stainless steels, aluminums, hi-temp alloys, and composites. Lasers can cut up to .500 inch thick in most metals.

What exactly is laser cutting? Lasers cut by concentrating laser light energy on the surface of a material, which absorbs the laser energy and then melts or vaporizes in a narrow path. An assist gas is delivered through the nozzle coaxial as the laser beam removes the molten cut material during the cut.

Elements of Laser Cutting

For the most successful and cost-effective laser cutting, a number of steps are necessary. First, a

Clean Cut™ is a trademark of U.S. Amada, Ltd.

laser program (tool path) is generated. It is possible to work from drawings, mylars, CAD/CAM information, existing parts, or templates.

Second, laser parameters — critical to achieve optimum cutting conditions — are set.

Material	Laser Cut/Max. Thickness	Clean Cut/Max. Thickness
Stainless Steel	.500"	.187"
Aluminum	.250"	.125"
Nickel-based Alloys	.310"	.187"
Titanium	.250"	.187"

Maximum material thickness capabilities of 1,500-watt CO_2 laser cutting versus 1,500-watt clean cutting are shown here.

Variables such as cutting speeds, laser power, laser mode, laser spot size, distance of cutting nozzle to the workpiece, and assist gases/pressure are carefully set.

The speed of laser cutting can be up to several hundred inches per minute. The power level most routinely used in CO_2 processing ranges from 50 to 5,000 watts.

Cutting occurs in two mode types — pulsed and continuous wave (CW) mode. In pulsed mode, typically used in welding and hole drilling, the electronic current discharged is switched on and off. In CW mode, routinely used for cutting, the laser is kept on for the duration of processing.

The spot size of the laser beam used for cutting is a key variable in laser processing. Spot sizes for high-power CO_2 cutting range from .004 inch to .006 inch. This enables the laser to cut with a kerf width of about .005 inch, keeping the amount of material lost during cutting to a minimum.

It is critical to keep the cutting nozzle at a constant distance from the material, with the beam focused on the surface or into the surface of material as determined by the application. Assist gases typically used include argon, helium, compressed air, nitrogen, and oxygen, all of which enhance the cutting results while blowing away molten material.

The Clean Cut Technique

What is the Clean Cut technique? This term describes a laser cutting process developed primarily for the aerospace and other commercial/industrial manufacturing operations that require a clean, oxide-free, weld-ready edge. Aerospace industries are concerned about what happens when heat from a laser is introduced to a laser-cut edge.

Users of high-power CO_2 lasers may unknowingly compromise a material being cut by leaving an edge structurally weakened, sometimes to the extreme where a metal looks like it was flame-cut. Laser clean cutting preserves the integrity of the material's edge.

To minimize the heat input to a part's edge and achieve a clean cut, a high-power CO_2 laser (1,500 watts or more) is used with a high rate of cutting speed, a high-pressure lens assembly, a high-pressure assist gas, and specific parameters.

When cutting as quickly as possible using a high-pressure assist gas such as nitrogen, the vaporized material is blown away quickly, which keeps the part cool by minimizing the time it is exposed to laser heat. Many metals can be Clean Cut up to .200 inch in thickness.

Typically, laser-cut parts are examined for edge conditions of microcracking, recast, and heat-affected zones (HAZs). Microcracking, defined metallurgically as microcracks penetrating into the parent material from the laser-cut edge, can be virtually eliminated when using the Clean Cut process.

Recast layer — the layer of metal adjacent to the melted cut edge — is usually less than .0005 inch when the Clean Cut process is used. HAZ is the metal between the recast layer and base material that exhibits grain structure changes. HAZ rarely exceeds .005 inch with clean cutting.

Many companies use laser cutting as a final trim process. However, in some cases, only net trimming can be used. If laser-cut parts require post cleanup, there are several options.

One option is that parts can be chemically etched. For example, SuperPlastic Forming (SPF) titanium parts are chemically etched to remove "alpha case" introduced by the SPF process. Etching also removes the heat-affected edge. Another option, mechanical cleanup of laser-cut edges, is also widely used. This can be accomplished through machining, benching, grinding, and hand-finishing.

Implementing Lasers in Manufacturing

A number of key steps must be taken to use laser cutting effectively. First, companies need to identify their own potential laser applications. Good laser processing candidates include parts that have small- to medium-volume runs, complex shapes, and which require clean, burr-free, weld-ready edges.

Second, if the application is critical in regard to microcracking, recast, and HAZ, "coupons" must be cut of the same type of material and thicknesses which mirror potential applications.

Third, metallurgical testing of the laser-cut edge needs to be done. Other types of testing may also be performed, such as stress, fatigue, and hardness testing.

Fourth, upon completion of testing, acceptable limits in regard to microcracking, recast, and HAZ must be determined and established.

Finally, a laser cutting specification must be written which incorporates not only the process specification, or laser schedule, but specific quality requirements for an acceptable laser-cut edge. Generally, potential applications may include noncritical, critical, and structural types of work.

Five-Axis Laser Cutting

Generally, the best processes for a five-axis laser include cutting, drilling, scribing and welding three-dimensional (3-D) shaped parts. Metal parts that are SPF, flow-formed, hydroformed, stamped, and deep drawn are obvious choices. Many composites are also five-axis compatible.

As a noncontact process, the benefits of this type of cutting include speed, accuracy, and a potential to Clean Cut complex parts. Current applications processed by five-axis lasers include jet engine components, ATF exhaust components, aerospace skins, wingspans, car and truck body parts, tank parts, aircraft interiors, appliance parts, aircraft combustion liners, sports equipment, and motorcycle fenders.

For example, one five-axis system is comprised of three linear axes (X,Y,Z) and two rotary axes (A,B) that are part of the robotic head. The sixth axis (C) is a capacity sensor that works as an independent axis. It is part of the robotic head that detects distance between the part and nozzle and adjusts for variations in the metal surface during cutting.

This feature is important in processing 3-D-type parts created through a variety of different forming processes. To meet high laser-cut standards, the cutting nozzle must be kept at a constant distance from the part to ensure consistent cutting conditions from one part to a run of parts.

Five-axis laser processing typically uses high-power CO_2 — 1,500 watts or more — and a large work envelope. The example system's envelope is 126 inches by 88 inches by 31.5 inches. The robotic controller, which can work in full five-axis in-space interpolation, is an alternative to CNC five-axis mechanically-driven systems.

To maintain a clean cutting environment, as well as protect expensive optical components, an exhaust system must be used to remove any fumes or particles left in the enclosure.

An enclosure with safety interlocked doors is needed to protect the operator and observers since the three linear axes, the robotic head, and the laser beam are all moving within the work envelope. Of course, access to the work enclosure must be prevented while the machine is operating.

The Beam Analyzer. The beam analyzer documents and enables exact duplication of processing parameters. Since changes in environment and deterioration of certain laser components do occur which impact power output, mode, and beam quality, parameters must be documented and adjusted to keep processing conditions constant and optimal.

The beam analyzer is the only way to ensure that the laser parameters used during the first successful run of parts will be duplicated on each subsequent run. This is accomplished by obtaining a printout of a set of key parameters measured at the output of the cutting nozzle.

Without knowing what the machine parameters are at the cutting nozzle, adjustment and duplication cannot be verified. The aerospace industry, like other precision manufacturing industries, requires the control, verification, and documentation of cutting parameters provided by the beam analyzer.

Fixturing. Mechanical lasers need complex tooling to the degree they move the part under a stationary laser head. However, with five-axis robotic systems, the part is tooled to stay in one place while the robotic head moves, so complex tooling is not needed. With these systems, most parts can be tooled to a table using either simple clamp or vacuum-type holding fixtures.

The key to fixturing five-axis parts effectively is to make sure that the part is supported, motion is prevented during processing, and the part is positioned for repeatability. Also, tooling must be designed to allow clearance for the cutting nozzle in tight cutting areas.

Teach Mode Programming. Programming for five-axis laser systems is based on a myriad of possible sources, including blueprints, CAD/CAM information, templates, check fixtures, mylars, scribed parts, and existing cut parts.

Since generating a five-axis program through conventional methods can be complicated and time-consuming, a simpler way to program a five-axis part was created. This programming approach is called the teach mode. It makes programming relatively easy, or user-friendly, because the operator can teach the computer the shape of the part and the cutting path.

What is the teach mode sequence? First, the operator fixtures the part. Second, a helium neon (HeNe) laser, which comes through the cutting nozzle, is used to follow along the part to teach the computer the shape of the part and the cut path. This information can also be generated from an off-line teach mode station.

Third, the information gained is then edited, if necessary. Finally, once a program is created, it is stored in the computer or on a floppy disk until further use. Thus, programming costs are nonrecurring.

Some systems allow the operator to program up to six different cutting modes. This capability is applicable in a situation where the operation goes from a mode of cutting straight sections to a mode of cutting in tight corners.

Case Study

A case study can illustrate what is typically requested of a laser job shop which uses both flat CO_2 cutters and a five-axis system.

One of the job shop's aerospace customers was manufacturing an aircraft nacelle (an enclosed part in an aircraft which houses the engine, cargo, etc.) using outdated technologies that required hand-processing. This was not only costly, but it also caused delivery problems.

The company's in-house process proceeded as follows: The part, made of .050-inch INCONEL® alloy material in coil form, was rolled out, and the cutting path was hand-scribed following a template. Then, using a large hand-held router, the part was rough cut — oversized by .125 inch — and hand-filed to the final shape required.

The part was then welded and bulge-formed into a cone shape. Next, it was sent back to be hand-scribed using an overlay template. The part was then cut out with a band saw, oversized again, and finally finished manually.

Some parts also required holes to be drilled, which was accomplished by using an overlay template with hole locations to accommodate a small hand drill.

By using laser processing, the company was able to eliminate this hand work. Clean cutting was used to bring the part to final dimensions with accuracy while reducing the part's total process time.

Using the laser flat cutters, a computer program was written on an off-line CAD/CAM sys-

INCONEL® is a trademark of the Inco family of companies.

tem, which nested the parts in a way to maximize use of a costly high-temperature alloy. Then, coils of material were Clean Cut to the final dimension, thereby eliminating hand-finishing.

The next steps of welding and bulge-forming were then completed. After bulge-forming, the cone was placed on the five-axis cutter. A simple holding fixture was used to trim the part to final dimensions (and laser drill holes, if required). Using the teach mode station, a program was quickly generated.

Finally, the part was Clean Cut — eliminating the need for secondary operations to prepare it for the next assembly.

In this case, the use of laser clean cutting improved quality and flow time and reduced cost. Yield was improved on high-temperature alloy materials by nesting parts. Process time for this part was reduced from ten to two hours per part while quality was improved on the final units.

Conclusion

What are the benefits of using five-axis laser cutting? First, it is a cost-effective process, provid-ing quality parts with repeatable accuracy. Second, it is a time-saving technique that reduces process flow-through time because of the minimal setup and tooling required. Third, the use of clean cutting minimizes the heat input to a part, keeps it distortion-free, and eliminates the need for secondary operations.

For many companies, the future of laser cutting is now. Laser cutting is being applied to various manufacturing processes, providing time-saving alternatives for those involved in state-of-the-art fabrication technologies. Many major aerospace, jet engine, and automotive companies are now either writing a laser specification in their quality control manuals or actually implementing laser processing into their manufacturing solutions.

If the present trend continues, the doors will open far wider to lasers in the manufacturing world in the next decade — especially since many of those doors quite possibly will have been cut by lasers.

Control of variables crucial to laser performance: A discussion of the factors affecting laser cut quality

About 15 years ago, the concept of laser cutting of sheet metal was introduced to the market. In the years since that introduction, the performance capability of sheet metal cutting lasers has steadily improved.

Much of this has been due to an improvement in the equipment, but a significant portion has also been due to an improved understanding of the variables which affect the quality of a laser cut and the ability to control those variables.

Only six or seven years ago, for instance, it was generally accepted that a laser is not a usable device for the production cutting of aluminum because of that metal's very poor absorption of energy at the 10.6 micrometer wave length of a CO_2 laser beam. Today, however, an excellent cut can be produced in ⅛-inch aluminum, for example, with a good surface finish and a minimal dross which flakes away easily.

The feed rate is about 25 inches per minute (IPM), which is acceptable for many manufacturing operations. Laser power for this cut is about 1,200 watts.

Laser power at this level has been available for several years; the new cutting capability is due to what has been learned about precise control of laser mode and focus, cutting speed, and the special application of inert assist gases.

Laser Beam

A piece of sheet metal can be cut with a beam of light because it is a very special type of light. Lasers have a "coherent" beam in which all of the light rays are moving parallel to one another and at the same wavelength. This makes it possible to focus the beam very precisely and to concentrate the full amount of energy available on a spot about .004 inch in diameter, thus generating enough heat to vaporize most materials.

When you used a magnifying glass to burn holes in leaves as a child, you had only random rays of the sun to work with and not a coherent beam of light. One basic variable in laser cutting is the effectiveness with which the laser resonator has aligned the rays of light or, in other words, the "purity" of the laser beam.

As a matter of fact, laser resonators do not put out an exactly parallel beam of light. The beam actually converges very slightly, but enough so that every beam has a "waist," which is a point at which it reaches a minimum diameter and then begins to diverge.

For this reason, most laser systems have a stated minimum distance between the exit of the laser beam from the resonator and the cutting point.

Also, in a so-called "full flying optics" system, in which the workpiece is stationary and the laser beam is moved around using mirrors, the beam length between resonator and cutting point is constantly varying, and the "waist" effect becomes a definite consideration.

Another basic variable with respect to beam quality is the mode. This refers to the distribution of energy across the laser beam. The ideal distribution is the basic TEM_{00} mode, which is a Gaussian pattern with a concentration of energy at the center. Some people compare a laser beam with this mode to a sharp knife.

An example of a different mode is the TEM_{01}, a doughnut-shaped distribution with energy concentrated around the rim of the focused spot. This type of beam is excellent for heat treating, but not ideal for cutting.

It is probably safe to say that any laser resonator on the market is capable of being tuned to deliver a near-perfect coherence and mode. The problem arises with stability. It is still a challenge to build a laser system in which — as power is varied from 0 to 100 percent, as ambient temperature changes, and as electrical and optical components age — the mode does not vary and the directional stability does not start to wander. Laser beam stability is a critical performance factor.

Table Motion

Common sense indicates that the quality of a laser cut is strongly influenced by how smoothly and accurately the material is moved around under the laser head (assuming this is a fixed-optics type of system)

The first obvious requirement is for rigidity in the table and in the drives, because any vibration transmitted from the surroundings or generated by the dynamic forces of table motion is going to show up as waviness in the cut edge. Similarly, the resolution of the control and the tightness of the feedback loop in the drives must be such that no irregularity in the cut path is discernable.

Probably the most demanding area of performance for the table and drives is the ability to get in and out of sharp corners. As the laser goes into an acute angle, the speed must ramp down to zero smoothly but sharply, then ramp up in the same way coming out of the corner. There should be no overshoot in the cut path, and at the same time there must be a minimum of dwell which will cause burning in the corner. Responsive, controlled acceleration and deceleration is another key performance requirement.

Assist Gases

Assist gases are of critical importance in laser cutting. Pure oxygen is used for cutting mild steel. Titanium must be shielded with an inert gas to control the cutting reaction. Selection of the proper assist gas or mixture of assist gases is therefore the first variable to be dealt with in this area.

Control of gas pressure, or more properly, the amount of gas fed to the process, is obviously important. With too little assist gas, the laser may not successfully cut the material. Too much gas can burn corners and put excess heat into the material.

The amount of assist gas required varies with the cutting feed rate. If the feed rate is severely changed, perhaps to slow down for a sharp corner, the gas pressure should change with it.

Recent work on processing difficult-to-cut materials has emphasized the importance of the flow of the assist gas. For best performance, the gas should be forced under considerable pressure down through the cut and out the other side to:

1. Provide gas assist through the whole depth of cut.

2. Carry away the waste particles so that they will not form dross on the under edge.

3. Provide cooling for the process.

Achieving this kind of flow is not easy. In the first place, the orifice in the nozzle must be narrowed down. This sharply increases the requirement for accuracy in alignment within the cutting head, so that the laser beam does not hit the edge of the nozzle.

Second, the nozzle must be brought down very close to the workpiece. This challenges the ability of the machine's mechanical or capacitative sensing system to follow closely the undulations of an uneven workpiece.

Finally, the shape of the interior cavity in the nozzle has to be carefully designed to eliminate turbulence and maintain a laminar flow of gas despite the conditions of high pressure and velocity.

Laser Power

Lasers used for sheet metal cutting are generally in the range of 500 watts to 1,500 watts. Higher power lasers are available and are used widely for applications such as welding and heat treating, but not too often for cutting. Below 1,500 watts or so, laser power and cutting capability tend to correspond fairly closely, but above this level additional laser power is quite expensive and may not return a comparable increase in cutting speed and cut quality.

Regardless of the maximum power rating, for almost all applications, a laser must be readily controllable from full power down to very low power levels and able to deliver a stable beam with good mode at low levels. Generally, for light-duty service, a smaller laser is better. For edge quality, the cuts produced by the early slow-flow 500-watt lasers are still the standard by which today's lasers are judged.

Power level can also be controlled by switching from continuous wave (CW) to pulsing mode, and then varying the width or the frequency of the pulses. Often, control of pulsing is the best way to achieve rapid and accurate variation in power level while retaining beam stability.

Most of today's lasers also have an enhanced pulsing capability which enables them to generate a pulse power level several times the normal rate for improved cutting in stainless steel and other difficult-to-cut materials.

Exhaust

Usually, the exhaust system is not thought of as a factor in the laser cutting process itself. However, a strong and effective exhaust will help in moving the assist gases through the cut and carrying away particles so that dross is not formed. A good exhaust system will also help keep lenses clean and free from splashback.

Interaction of Factors

Taken all together, the points described in this article make up a rather imposing list of variables, every one of which must be kept under control and some of which must be held within very tight limits to produce an acceptable laser cut. Adding to the difficulty, some of these factors have strong interactions with others.

The most critical of these interactions is probably the three-way relationship between feed rate, laser power level, and gas pressure. A significant change in one of these elements will require a variation in the other two.

Most often, this is seen when the feed rate has to be slowed because of the geometry being traced, and the laser power level and assist gas pressure must be correspondingly adjusted.

The relationships between these variables might be worked out for a particular material and thickness, but when we move to another set of conditions — a different material, perhaps, and maybe one which requires an inert assist gas — the relationships can be very different.

Although not as complex, the problem can almost be compared to that of a doctor prescribing a medication for the human system, when a desired result is often accompanied by all sorts of unexpected side effects.

Generally, however, the laser industry has made tremendous progress in recent years in understanding the variables which are important in the laser cutting of sheet metal. The effect of changes in the purity and stability of the laser beam, the need for structural rigidity and smooth dynamic response, the multiple critical functions of the assist gas, and the effect of varying power levels or of pulsing are all known.

Most importantly, the industry is now getting a handle on the interactions between these variables. This has allowed the striking improvements in laser cutting performance which have recently been achieved.

Reducing heat effect:
How to lessen thermal damage
in laser cut parts

Laser cutting of metals by its very nature creates a heat-affected zone (HAZ) along the boundaries of the cut region. HAZ refers to the portion of material that has undergone permanent thermal damage because of the cutting process. During continuous wave (CW) cutting, the typical HAZ for mild and stainless steels can range from .010 inch (.25 millimeter) to more than .040 inch (1 millimeter).

Heat-Affected Zone Comparison of CW and Pulsed Mild Steel			
Material Thickness (Gauge)	(Inch)	CW HAZ (Inch)	Pulsed HAZ (Inch)
8	0.164	0.020	0.006
11	0.120	0.015	0.006
14	0.075	0.042	0.005
20	0.036	0.030	0.003
24	0.024	0.024	0.002

The HAZ alters material properties. This can result in lower tensile strength, changes in material hardness, or increased porosity in welds. HAZ also produces cosmetic damage exhibited by material discoloration.

Though the advantages of laser processing — precision cutting and versatility in application — may outweigh the disadvantage of the resulting heat effect, the presence of a HAZ is of primary concern in many applications in which structural integrity is critical or the laser cut surface is visible. In aerospace and related industries, secondary machining operations are required to remove the HAZ. The added cost of these operations often warrants the use of traditional machining methods which are generally more cost-effective.

Pulsing to Reduce HAZ

To maintain accuracy on intricate contours, the cutting speed must be reduced. Reducing the feed rate only, however, will introduce additional heat to the part and result in melting, distortion, or increased HAZ of the workpiece. Thus, the part will lose definition because it has absorbed too much heat.

To maintain workpiece definition, it is critical to limit the amount of heat introduced to the part. The object is to reduce the heat for a given feed rate and achieve a balance among the feed rate, average power, and ejection of the molten material.

Pulsing, or gating, by turning the laser beam on and off reduces average power to the workpiece while maintaining high CW values and efficient coupling of the laser beam to the workpiece.

High energy levels given off for short periods of time allow coupling of material and impart the least amount of thermal damage to the workpiece, thus narrowing the HAZ. Pulsing allows intricate parts to be cut at lower feed rates to achieve definition. Although average power can be reduced by reducing the CW power, this in turn results in a loss of coupling efficiency. By pulsing, coupling efficiency is not sacrificed.

Pulsing of the laser beam can reduce the HAZ to typically less than .010 inch (.25 millimeter). In many instances, this reduction in HAZ can produce acceptable mechanical integrity and visually attractive edge quality.

Transverse flow lasers can have a mechanical chopper to duplicate gated pulsing. Limited to fast axial and slow-flow lasers, enhanced pulsing permits the laser to transmit a burst of energy for a brief length of time — usually hundreds of microseconds. The resulting peak pulse power is slightly higher than that of an average CW.

Although it ensures minimal thermal damage, pulsing reduces the average power and, hence, speed of cutting. Using a pulse schedule of one millisecond on and one millisecond off of the discharge current for a 1,200-watt laser renders an average power reading of 600 watts with a duty cycle of 50 percent.

While $1/16$-inch material may be cut in the CW mode at 250 inches per minute (IPM), pulsing of that same material would result in a reduced cutting speed of 120 IPM.

The duty cycle provides the average power. If duty cycle of 20 percent is achieved with 1,200 watts, average power equals approximately 240.

Pulsing allows you to use the versatility of the laser punch press combination and the control to full advantage to get the required part and desired accuracy in the fastest possible time. Pulsing increases versatility and the production of good quality cuts.

When to Pulse

Use pulsing when cutting material at a feed rate lower than the feed rate that could be realized with CW. The goal is to achieve and retain fine definition of the part. If the maximum feed rate cannot be achieved because of loss of part accuracy or definition, use pulse.

Pulsing should be used only in instances when the workpiece requires intricate contouring and the motion system cannot travel at a speed fast enough to provide an accurate cut in the CW mode. For instance, in the cutting of a circular saw blade, most motion systems cannot handle the 200 to 250 IPM speed needed to generate an accurate part. In this case, use pulsing for complex contouring, then CW for the majority of the cutting.

Pulsing is not generally an advantage when cutting aluminum, brass, and copper. To overcome the high thermal conductivity of these materials, average power must be increased. In the pulsing operation, average power is reduced, which in turn reduces the heating effect of the workpiece.

Enhanced Pulsing

Many lasers can now be equipped with an enhanced pulsing feature that is also known as Superpulsing. Enhanced pulsing allows the generation of bursts of power many times the standard CW level.

Developed for the processing of super alloys and, specifically, to address the concerns of the aerospace industry — which requires parts with little or no HAZ — Superpulsing generates very high peak energies and low average power, generally at a feed rate one-tenth the normal cutting speed. Peak power achieved by enhanced pulsing is, on average, three times that of rated CW power.

Superpulsing is used for cutting materials that generally produce dross such as refractory alloys and stainless steels. For example, Superpulsing may be used in the production of air compressor valve plates which require very sharp corners, good edge quality, and minimal burr.

Superpulsing operates using even less average power than pulsing. However, Superpulsing lends fine control of the average power imparted to the workpiece. An enhancement in the output power per pulse improves coupling efficiency.

Superpulsing provides very fine control of the part, no loss of coupling efficiency, and almost no heat effect. The limitation of average power means the Superpulsing operation is very low.

Improving laser cutting quality in humid weather: How to beat cooled optics condensation

Mother nature and weather are hard to beat, both good and bad, but of all human-kind's attempts to modify weather, probably the most effort has been and is directed toward the control of humidity.

Although metal fabrication shops range from those with clean room conditions to those with gravel floors and no walls, sophisticated laser metal cutting systems are expected to perform reliably at all times, regardless of ambient conditions.

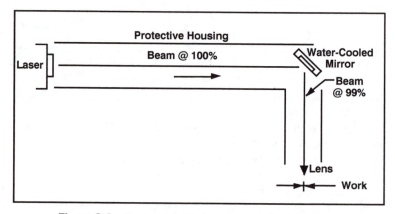

Figure 8-1. The bending of a laser beam is illustrated here.

CO$_2$ System Design

Why should humidity be a problem when cutting materials with high-power CO$_2$ lasers? Look at the cutting system configuration first. For the CO$_2$ laser to be used for cutting, it is necessary to "bend the beam," no matter what type of complex motion system is used for either the beam or the workpiece.

When it meets the workpiece to cut, the CO$_2$ beam is generally at right angles to its discharge from the resonator/oscillator assembly, also know as the laser.

Bending the beam requires at least one mirror or optic component (see **Figure 8-1**). This mirror, acting together with a lens, then focuses the beam on the work accurately enough for the cutting process. Generally, for the higher-power systems, this mirror is designed to be water-cooled.

The mirror is coated with a material selected for high efficiency, over 99 percent reflection at a 45-degree angle. Even though the laser output is stable, the condition and cleanliness of the mirror coating will affect the quality (mode) and consistency of the beam. A slight distortion of the mirror surface will dramatically alter the beam.

The mode is extremely important to edge quality on many materials and it is always a factor in the cutting speed.

Any foreign material or film, such as condensation residue on the mirror coating, reduces its efficiency and shortens the mirror life. Repeated exposure to condensation coupled with normal airborne materials will cause the mirror to overheat, eventually leading to complete failure.

The lens is also impacted by contamination, but the mirror is the most sensitive component in the external beam delivery network.

The Problem with Condensation

Now comes the psychometrics (the science of water vapor in the air) part of the problem. Everyone knows how a glass of cold beverage sweats (condenses) during warm weather, and that if the condensation is left to dry, it leaves residue. The same holds true for the cooled optics.

The mirror is designed to absorb only a small percentage of the beam, but that still translates into measurable heat. So, it must be cooled, because too much heat will damage the mirror. Remember, the more residue there is, the more heat is absorbed by the substrate of the mirror.

It seems like a "Catch 22" situation. Why, if the mirror is warm, should it sweat? It is because the beam is not always on and providing heat, but the water flow is on, providing cooling.

When one considers just the time it takes to load the work on the system table, it is not surprising that condensation develops repeatedly.

Figure 8-2 shows examples of safe cooling water temperatures above which condensation will not form for various relative humidity and air temperature combinations.

The television weather person is a good source for relative humidity information if the desire is to adjust the cooling temperatures daily. However, if

Recommended Temperature Settings Based on Outside Temperature and Relative Humidity Conditions			
Outside Temperature Degrees F	Outside Relative Humidity %	Dewpoint Temperature Degrees F	Optimum Temperature to Laser Degrees F
70	70	59	61
	80	63	65
	90	67	69
75	60	61	63
	70	64	66
	80	69	71
	90	72	74
80	50	59	61
	60	65	67
	70	69	71
	80	73	75
	90	77	79
85	50	65	67
	60	69	71
	70	75	77
	80	79	81
	90	81	83
90	40	63	65
	50	68	70
	60	74	76
	70	79	81
95	30	59	61
	40	67	69
	50	71	73
	60	79	81
	70	83	85
100	30	63	65
	40	72	74
	50	78	80
	60	83	85
	70	89	91

© Optitemp Inc.

Figure 8-2. Above these cooling water temperatures, condensation will not form for various relative humidity and air temperature combinations.

a temperature based on historical weather data is selected, it is possible to keep that temperature constant, just as the laser cooling temperature is held constant.

Cold Water

What should a laser operator do, since the laser requires cooling at a precise temperature, usually 65 degrees Fahrenheit (19 degrees Celsius), and the same cooling water source is generally used for the optics cooling water as well?

If the water temperature for the laser is lower than the temperature called for in Figure 8-2, considerable condensation will form. If the laser cooling temperature is raised, the laser could overheat, and repairing it can be a major expense.

A Solution

One answer is to provide two temperatures of cooling water, just as most laser designs are now requiring. The cooling loads for optics are as small as a light bulb in some cases, and the flows, although critical, are small as well.

It should be safe to assume that the water chiller or other cooling water source is already removing the heat from the optics circuit, so there is enough cooling capacity to provide a heat sink for the second circuit.

All that is required for a second temperature is the addition of a pre-engineered water-to-water heat exchanger, digital controller, and pump assembly (if controlled temperatures are desired, which they are), or simply a radiator and pump arrangement (if a variable temperature is judged sufficient).

Should a shop really spend money for something so simple, when it is only humid for a few days each year? Even air-conditioned shops find it necessary to control optics temperature to maximize production time.

The time and quality lost in one problem episode more than offsets the cost of the equipment involved in setting up a second circuit, not to mention the replacement cost of the optics components as a cost justification.

The Bottom Line

The bottom line is: what does it cost *not* to do it? Have setup parameters ever been off the mark on some days? Has edge quality dropped during a production run? Has it ever been necessary to slow down to cut at all? Has the system been shut down to troubleshoot those symptoms?

"Yes" answers to these questions cost money, not to mention repeat orders and, perhaps, customers. It seems logical to eliminate Mother Nature from one's fortunes, if possible, by adding controlled cooling to laser optics.

New developments
in laser fusion cutting

Conventional laser cutting with low gas pressures imposes some limitations on the quality of the cutting process and the further processing of cut components. With stainless steel and low-carbon steel parts, an oxide layer forms by the reaction with oxygen during the exothermic process. Aluminum parts can be cut with either oxygen or nitrogen, but both methods can cause surface quality difficulties and burr development.

Stainless Steel. When cutting stainless steel, the oxygen layer has a two-fold effect:

1. Its presence disturbs the corrosion resistance in the immediate vicinity of the cutting edge. A rust layer several millimeters wide forms at the surface from an exposure to corrosive elements.

2. If untreated cutting edges are welded, the quality of the weld is inadequate — it is porous and beset with joint flaws.

Low-Carbon Steel. This material is not corrosion-resistant itself, so the oxide layer is of little significance in regards to corrosion. Also, the weldability of the material is satisfactory with an untreated laser cut edge quality. A problem area here is during after-process painting, because paint often adheres poorly to oxidized surfaces.

Aluminum. Cutting aluminum with oxygen results in a very rough cutting surface and a burr at the bottom of the kerf. This burr results from the solidification of aluminum oxides, which have a higher melting point than the base material. However, this burr can be easily removed because it is very brittle.

Using nitrogen as an assist gas improves the edge quality. The chemical reaction forming aluminum oxides does not occur. Still, with material thicknesses greater than 1 millimeter, a burr builds up — in this case consisting of pure aluminum — that is difficult to remove.

Possible Solutions

Several alternatives to conventional cutting techniques involve single, low-pressure assist gases:

1. Cutting with a dual gas flow to use the exothermic reaction of the material with oxygen and to create a protective shield on the cutting edge. This process has shown some positive results when cutting aluminum.

2. Cutting with inert gases at very high pressures. This process, called fusion cutting, has shown good results on all three materials (aluminum, stainless steel, and low-carbon steel).

Types of Laser Cutting

This section describes the difference between laser fusion cutting and conventional laser cutting

Laser Oxygen Cutting. The laser beam needs to heat up the metal to ignition temperature, producing a defined cut in the oxygen stream. The exothermic reaction heat increases the energy supply, raising the cutting speeds by a factor of approximately two to four above that of fusion cutting.

This method achieves the highest working speed of all laser cutting processes. Because of these high process speeds, oxygen is used to cut most steels.

Laser Fusion Cutting. Instead of the oxygen as cutting gas, this process makes use of an inert gas such as nitrogen, argon, or helium. The laser beam melts the material, while the gas jet drives

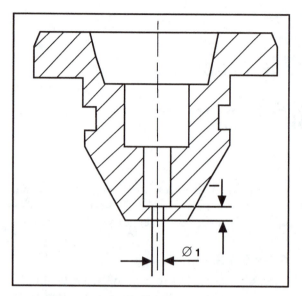

Figure 9-1. This diagram shows a 1-millimeter diameter standard nozzle with a cylindrical length of 1 millimeter.

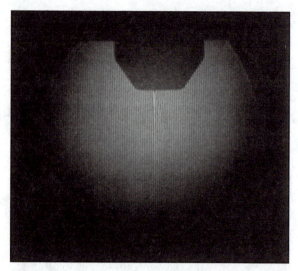

Figure 9-2. The exposures from the interferometric examination of the gas jet showed that the flow after the nozzle opening occurred without disturbances at high gas pressures.

the liquified material from the cut. The cutting speed is reduced by the absence of exothermic combustion energy contribution and the poor absorption of the beam energy at the cutting front[1].

At material thicknesses above 1 to 2 millimeters, burrs often form on the lower side of the cut. To make laser fusion cutting suitable for manufacturing, this burr formation must be eliminated. This can be done by addressing the gas flow. One solution is to raise the cutting gas pressure to values of up to 15 bar. This can improve liquified material clearing enough to safely suppress the adherence of burrs. However, this measure alone is not always adequate for consistent cutting in practical operation.

Requirements for Fusion Cutting

To provide the basics for a consistently reliable laser fusion cutting process, components of the beam delivery system must be modified and adapted for the use of high-pressure gases. These components include the gas nozzle, the optics, height sensing, and the basic machine concept.

Adapted Nozzle Shape. Cutting tests on high-grade steel plates, 2 and 3 millimeters thick

respectively, were conducted with a 1-millimeter diameter standard nozzle with a cylindrical length of 1 millimeter (see **Figure 9-1**).

Cuts without burrs were achieved when the distance between the nozzle and plate was smaller than 0.2 millimeter and the minimum gas pressure was 14 bar. This short distance can cause difficulties in practice. Without a capacitive distance control, it is very difficult to maintain a consistent gap of this magnitude. Working a height sensor with a distance of 0.2 millimeter can cause problems when fine spatter is occasionally thrown up over the plate surface. The control consequently increases the cutting distance, and the result is an incomplete cut.

In addition, such a short distance leads to rapid nozzle wear and deteriorating cutting quality. For this reason, nozzle shapes had to be found which permitted greater working distances. Nozzles were designed for 10 bar and 15 bar cutting gas pressure. Their conical openings resulted in the formation of an ultrasonic flow. The formation of the gas jet was interferometrically examined, and the exposures showed that the flow after the nozzle

[1]Petring, Abels, Beyer, and Herziger, "Cutting of metallic materials with CO_2 high-performance lasers," Feinwerktechnik & Messtechnik 9/88.

opening occurred without disturbances at these high gas pressures (see **Figure 9-2**).

The effects on the cutting result were established in cutting tests with both nozzle shapes adapted to 10 and 15 bar. The most important characteristic of these nozzles was that the improved output allowed improved coupling of gas in the cutting gap, permitting an increase of the distance from the nozzle to the sheet surface. The distance could be increased to 1 millimeter with perfect cutting quality.

Optics. Typical assist gas pressures for oxygen cutting have a maximum level of 5 bar, depending on the application. Transmissive optics with a standard thickness can resist such pressures, but not much higher forces. In testing, since laser fusion cutting applies gas pressures up to 15 bar, optics had to be chosen that were significantly thicker than the original ones used. This minimized distortion in the optics caused by the higher pressures on the optic's surface.

Machine Concepts. The higher gas pressures not only influence the design of the optics, but also increase the forces put on the workpiece. Thinner sheets especially have a tendency to give way under the pressure and move out of focus. Some machine types are more suitable than others to overcome these difficulties:

1. A flying optics flat bed cutter should incorporate a sufficient number of ribs in its table to support the sheet properly. A height sensor is needed to keep the gap between gas nozzle and material constant.

2. A five-axis machine also needs a height sensor, but when working on formed material, the strength of the workpiece is usually sufficient to withhold the gas forces.

Distance Nozzle Plate 0.8 mm						
Material: Stainless Steel 18% Cr 10% Ni Cutting Gas: Nitrogen						
		P = 1,500 W			P = 1,000 W	
Thickness	Feed	Pressure	Focus	Feed	Pressure	Focus
1 mm	7	6	-0.4	5.2	6	-0.4
2 mm	4	7	-1.2	2.7	8	-1.2
3 mm	2.3	9	-2.1	1.3	12	-2.3
4 mm	1.3	12	-3.1	0.7	15	-3.5
5 mm	0.9	15	-6.0			

Figure 9-3. This table shows the cutting results with the adapted high-pressure nozzle.

Figure 9-4. The cross sections of optimized cuts all show a characteristic widening of the kerf in the upper area.

3. A machine with a fixed focusing head and a material motion system for the sheet works very well, because the sheet is constantly supported from the bottom around the funnel extracting the cutting fumes.

The machines should also be able to perform axis accelerations larger than 5 meters per second squared to avoid the formation of burrs.

Establishing the Cutting Parameters

Position of the Focal Point. During the cutting parameter optimization, the focal position had to be adjusted differently than for laser oxygen cutting. In laser oxygen cutting, the focus is

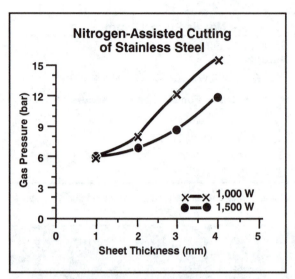

Figure 9-5. The relation between the required cutting gas pressure for burr-free cuts, the material thickness, and the laser output power is shown here.

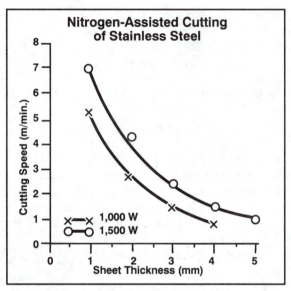

Figure 9-6. Pictured here is the feed rate as a function of the sheet thickness.

usually on the sheet surface for thicknesses below 6 millimeters. For fusion cutting, the focus has to be deeper into the plate to guarantee a burr-free cut (see **Figure 9-3**). This way, the kerf is made wider, facilitating the clearing of molten material, while the lower focal position results in a better laser beam illumination on the lower section of the cutting form[1]. Consequently the liquefying temperature is increased in this critical area.

The cross sections of the optimized cuts all show a characteristic widening of the kerf in the upper area (see **Figure 9-4**), supporting the assumption of an improved gas throughput. With lower focal positions of more than 3 millimeters below the plate surface, the narrowest cross section of the nozzle (1-millimeter diameter) can lead to a chopping of the laser beam, so the nozzle diameter for the test had to be increased.

Materials and Thicknesses. The materials that have been cut successfully so far with high-pressure inert gases are stainless steels (mainly 300 series), aluminum (AlMg and AlMgSi alloys), galvanized steels, low-carbon steels, and titanium. Maximum sheet thickness for stainless steel and aluminum is 5 millimeters for a burr-free cut.

Figure 9-5 shows the relation between the required cutting gas pressure for burr-free cuts, the material thickness, and the laser output power. With increased laser performance, a smaller gas impulse is sufficient to avoid burr adherence.

Feed Rates. In **Figure 9-6**, the feed rate is shown as a function of the sheet thickness. An important distinguishing feature when compared with the oxygen cutting is that burrs are formed not only when the maximum cutting speed is exceeded, but also if the feed rate falls below a minimum speed. This minimum speed limit is approximately two thirds of the maximum speed. Below this speed, a very pronounced burr is formed.

This behavior places higher demands on the dynamics of the guiding machine. For instance, on machines with low axis accelerations, burr formations can be initiated at every contour transition. At acceleration values of 5 meters per second squared and more, this problem can no longer be noticed.

The feed rates with laser fusion cutting are slower than feedrates achievable with oxygen-assisted cuts. **Figure 9-7** compares the cutting speeds of both processes. Up to 70 percent of the feed rates achieved with laser oxygen cutting

[1]*Petring, Abels, Beyer, and Herziger, "Cutting of metallic materials with CO_2 high-performance lasers," Feinwerktechnik & Messtechnik 9/88.*

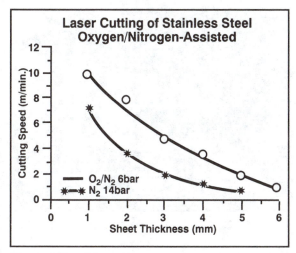

Figure 9-7. This graph compares the cutting speeds of laser fusion cutting and oxygen-assisted cutting.

Figure 9-8. A cross section of a weld sample cut with high-pressure inert gas is shown here.

Figure 9-9. This is a weld sample cut with oxygen.

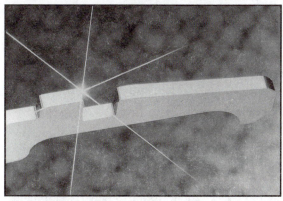

Figure 9-10. The cutting edge of a 4-millimeter thick stainless steel plate is pictured here.

can be reached with fusion cutting in thinner materials. In thicker materials, this ratio drops to 30 percent or less.

Oxygen Cutting versus Fusion Cutting

Corrosion Tests. In corrosion tests, no rust formed at the cutting edge when fusion cutting stainless steel, while comparative samples cut with oxygen started to rust within the testing period.

Welding Tests. As known from earlier tests, the oxide layer on the cutting edge leads to the formation of pores during subsequent welding. To compare the welding result of the steel plates cut with different methods, laser cut edges were laser welded without further preparation after the cutting process.

A cross section of a weld sample cut with high-pressure inert gas is shown in **Figure 9-8**. The weld was free of porosity and did not show any flaws. A sample cut with oxygen is displayed in **Figure 9-9**. This weld had frequent pores, and some parts were not cleanly joined at the root of the weld.

Edge Quality. The cutting edge of a 4-millimeter thick stainless steel plate is shown in **Figure 9-10**. As shown, the plate underside does not show any burr adherence at all. The cut surface is metallically bare and is, therefore, suitable for any form of

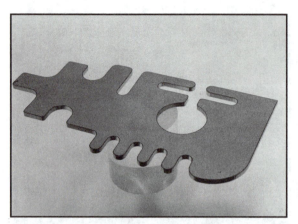

Figure 9-11. Laser fusion cutting can produce surfaces with very little roughness.

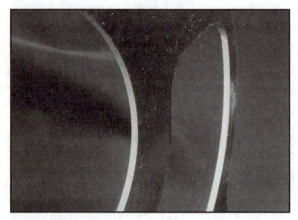

Figure 9-12. Burr-free cuts can be achieved with laser fusion cutting.

further processing. This is valid for all materials that have been sampled so far. The surface roughness was decreased, especially in the samples of aluminum and stainless steel.

Economy. Although advantages to laser fusion cutting have been shown, it must be noted that two cost factors make it more expensive than laser oxygen cutting. First, laser fusion cutting consumes a considerable amount of gas, especially when cutting thicker materials. Also, the working speed is slower than laser oxygen cutting.

These factors must be compared with the savings achieved by elimination of reworking. Small components, which can easily be cleaned in the pickling bath, require less work than large components, from which the oxide layer usually must be removed manually.

Samples. As shown, laser fusion cutting can produce surfaces with very little roughness (see **Figure 9-11**), burr-free cuts (see **Figure 9-12**), and sharp corners and edges because of a small heat-affected zone (HAZ) (see **Figure 9-13**).

Future Applications and Developments

Fusion cutting opens up a new field of applications for some materials that were difficult to cut with CO_2 lasers until now. Manufacturers that process a large quantity of stainless steels or aluminum could benefit from this new development. For more exotic materials, like the ones typically

Figure 9-13. Laser fusion cutting can result in sharp corners and edges because of a small HAZ.

used in the aerospace industry, research will be done to evaluate the laser fusion cutting technique. The automotive and appliance industry will probably be looking at applications involving galvanized materials.

Future research and development efforts will focus on improving the process parameters to make the process more competitive and to produce comparable quality when cutting thicker materials. Therefore, further improvements in the nozzle configuration will be investigated, and greater laser powers with a high-quality mode structure must be developed.

Chapter 3 Thermal Cutting

Cutting with precision plasma technology: Stabilized jet helps improve cut quality

Today's competitive climate requires that fabricators produce better products at lower cost. One important way to achieve this is to cut component parts and shapes to tighter tolerances that require less finishing work. Until recently, the only choice has been laser cutting.

Although the conventional plasma cutting process offers a more efficient and cost-effective method, its physical nature keeps it from satisfying the quality and precision requirements.

In the last decade, extensive research has been done to find a better way to stabilize and control this energy. This has resulted in the development of the precision plasma process.

This article describes precision plasma cutting and compares it with the laser process. It also discusses the type of machines with which the technology can be used. Since computer control is important in achieving high performance with the precision plasma process, the role of computer-aided manufacturing (CAM) integration is also discussed. Finally, the article reviews some case histories and actual user experience.

Shape Cutting Processes

Energy in the form of laser light can be focused optically to produce a high density in a small area. Enough energy can be focused and delivered to that spot on a piece of steel to actually heat the steel to the temperature at which it will melt and burn.

For thicknesses of steel within a certain range, this maintains a beam-like cutting action, resulting in a high-quality edge and a very precise, narrow kerf.

In the conventional plasma arc cutter, an electric arc is established from an electrode inside the torch tip. The arc passes through a nozzle opening to the metal being cut, and the electric energy ionizes the gas blown into this arc. The ionized gas leaves the torch in the form of a high-velocity jet, and it releases a tremendous amount of energy in the form of heat.

In this form, the gas is called **plasma**. This extremely hot jet cuts through the metal by melting and burning it. This jet does not have the beam-like characteristic of the laser. It is a simple

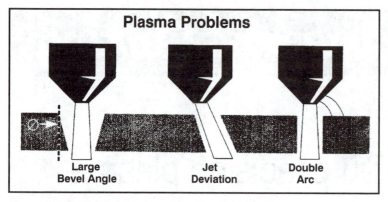

Figure 10-1. The three main problems associated with conventional plasma are illustrated here.

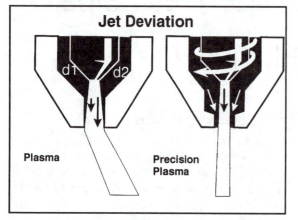

Figure 10-2. Minute differences in concentricity between the electrode and the nozzle create pressure differences across the orifice, deflecting the plasma jet as it leaves the nozzle.

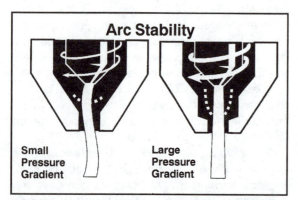

Figure 10-3. When the vortex develops a large pressure gradient in the chamber, the arc and jet are constricted, stabilizing the plasma.

yet powerful process which, unfortunately, is very difficult to control.

Arc temperatures inside the torch range upwards from 17,000 degrees Celsius. As the jet blasts through the material, it produces a wide kerf which has considerable variation and bevel angle at the cut edge, affecting the precision of the part. In addition, some of the molten material recasts itself on the bottom of the edge, creating hard-to-remove dross. Finally, the electrode and nozzle erode at a fairly high rate and must be replaced often.

The three main problems associated with conventional plasma are (see **Figure 10-1**):

1. A large bevel angle which can vary considerably over the life of the nozzle.

2. Significant pressure variation across the opening of the orifice because of the stresses created by the process. This variation causes the jet to deviate to the side, affecting the precision of the cut part.

3. A tendency for double arcing, reducing the efficiency of the process and shortening the life of the nozzle and electrode.

The Precision Plasma Process

How are these problems addressed with precision plasma technology?

First, consider jet deviation. Minute differences in concentricity between the electrode and the nozzle create pressure differences across the orifice (see **Figure 10-2**). This deflects the plasma jet as it leaves the nozzle.

Also, in the case of conventional plasma, the magnitude of the tangential gas velocity is very small. This maintains only a small pressure gradient across the nozzle. Attempts to increase the tangential velocity will destabilize the process because of the geometry.

To deal with these arc and plasma jet instabilities, a high-velocity mixing chamber has been designed that equalizes the flow pressure before the plasma

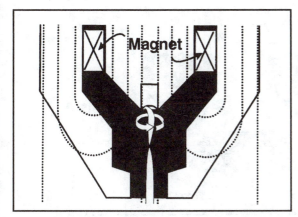

Figure 10-4. A magnetic field has been introduced to help improve the productivity of a mechanically-stabilized plasma jet.

leaves the nozzle. Increasing the tangential component of the gas velocity with a gas swirler creates a vortex similar to a tornado. This vortex develops a large pressure gradient (see **Figure 10-3**) in the chamber, constricting the arc and jet.

Through these mechanical means, the plasma can be somewhat stabilized, resulting in improved cut edge quality. Also, by increasing the energy density, most of the dross problem is eliminated.

On the other hand, these improvements are not gained without compromise. Increasing the energy density beyond certain low values becomes difficult. This produces the undesirable effect of reduced cutting speed and efficiency. So, while cut quality and kerf width predictability have been improved — creating more precision — productivity has been reduced

A new plasma system addresses this productivity barrier. When the plasma arc flows through the orifice, it conducts an electric current and is subject to Lorentz forces — the same forces that control an electric motor and make it spin. To overcome the productivity compromise produced by mechanically stabilizing the plasma jet, a magnetic field has been introduced (see **Figure 10-4**).

This magnetic field has two primary effects:

1. The Lorentz forces acting on the plasma arc itself make it spin faster and more tightly on the tip of the electrode. This keeps the point of arc con-

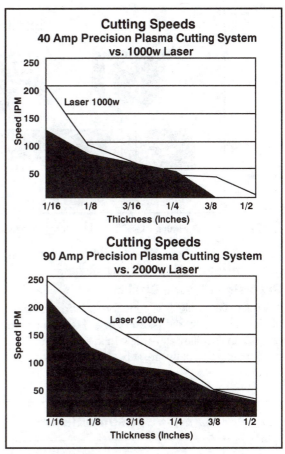

Figure 10-5. Precision plasma system cutting speed ranges are shown here as a function of thickness compared with typical laser speed ranges.

tact in constant motion, increasing the life of the electrode.

2. The magnetic field lines trap the spinning plasma, reducing the risk of deviation and double arcing as it leaves the nozzle. Thus, stability is maintained even as the energy levels are increased.

The system can produce a very narrow kerf at high cutting speeds. For example, the cross-sectional area of the nozzle can be about one-tenth that of a conventional plasma nozzle.

Precision Plasma Cutting Speeds

Precision plasma systems are available with powers of 40 amps and 90 amps. **Figure 10-5** shows

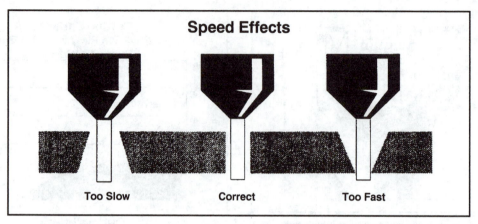

Figure 10-6. The bevel angle is a function of the precision plasma cutting speed.

cutting speed ranges as a function of thickness compared with typical laser speed ranges.

Precision Plasma Quality

The bevel angle is a function of the precision plasma cutting speed (see **Figure 10-6**). For example, in 9-millimeter-thick mild steel, the best quality range is between 0.5 and 1.0 meters per minute.

Precision Plasma Operating Costs

The major operating cost of the precision plasma system is the replacement of consumable parts. The number of pierces and cutting arc time affect the life of the electrode and nozzle (see **Figure 10-7**), and the operating cost is predictable under various circumstances.

For example, after 400 pierces and a little more than five hours of arc time, the consumables should be replaced. However, in an application involving only two hours of arc time, more than 500 pierces can be made.

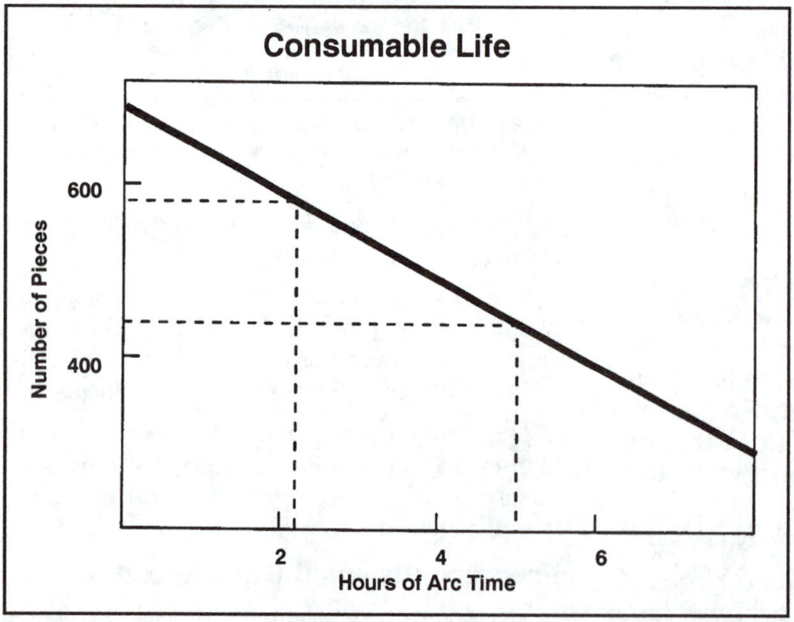

Much of the energy used in conventional plasma is absorbed by the metal, which can cause deformation. A test part was used to measure the heat deformation (see **Figure 10-8**). When the part was cut with the precision plasma system, the distortion was minimal and similar to laser cutting results.

In the same regard, since most of the heat is used efficiently in the cutting process, hardening results (see **Figure 10-9**) are also similar to those produced by laser cutting.

Figure 10-7. In precision plasma cutting, the number of pierces and cutting arc time affect the life of the electrode and nozzle.

Machine Systems

Conventional plasma cutting machines are not acceptable for precision plasma cutting since they do not provide a smooth, accurate platform.

In the cantilever construction of the conventional plasma cutting machine, the far side of the beam has a drive system, while the near side of the beam simply floats or has a roller supporting its weight (see **Figure 10-10**).

As the beam accelerates or decelerates during contouring, the floating side has a tendency to swing about or lag behind the driven side. This can produce variable results, particularly when parts are compared from one side of the table to the other.

With a gantry design (see **Figure 10-11**), the torch may be moved in one axis along a fixed beam while the sheet is moved in the other axis. For heavier material and larger sheet sizes, it is generally more practical to move the torch on the beam for one axis and then move the beam for the other axis.

Both sides of the beam are captured on fixed machine ways. Each side can be driven independently, but this is only acceptable at very low speeds because of synchronization difficulties.

Improved performance results when rack and pinion drive is used on both sides of the machine (see **Figure 10-12**), if the pinions are at the ends of a single drive shaft and locked together. This prevents any nonsynchronous motion or yawing. The shaft is driven at the center by a single motor.

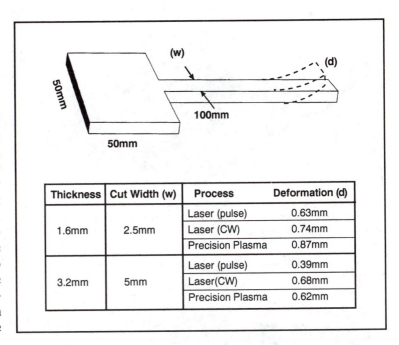

Thickness	Cut Width (w)	Process	Deformation (d)
1.6mm	2.5mm	Laser (pulse)	0.63mm
		Laser (CW)	0.74mm
		Precision Plasma	0.87mm
3.2mm	5mm	Laser (pulse)	0.39mm
		Laser(CW)	0.68mm
		Precision Plasma	0.62mm

Figure 10-8. This is a test part that was used to measure the heat deformation of conventional and precision plasma.

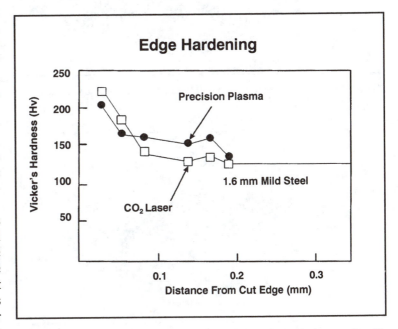

Figure 10-9. In the same regard as heat deformation, hardening results with precision plasma are similar to those produced by laser cutting.

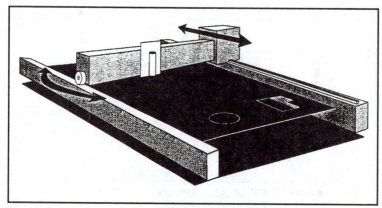

Figure 10-10. In a cantilever machine system, the far side of the beam has a drive system, while the near side of the beam floats or has a roller supporting its weight.

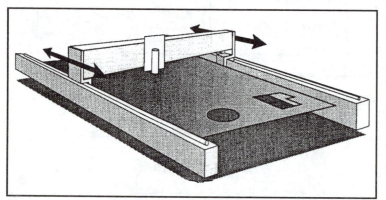

Figure 10-11. In the gantry design, both sides of the beam are captured on fixed machine ways.

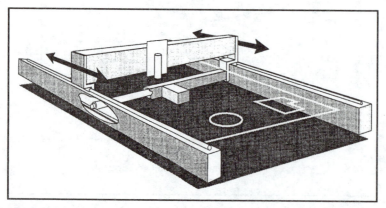

Figure 10-12. Dual-side rack and pinion helps improve performance on a plasma cutting machine.

Machine Accuracy

A laser interferometer can be used to verify machine positioning accuracy. A computer controls the machine, and the laser is used to measure any error in the desired position. This is done for both sides of the machine over the entire length of travel, and across the beam as well. For this static test the machine is allowed to come to rest as the measurements are taken.

To determine how the machine will perform under cutting conditions, the deviation must be measured from the desired contour path while in motion. Using methods described in ANSI B5.54, a ball socket is fixed to the table, and another socket — joined to the first with a telescoping measurement device — is mounted in the torch holder (see **Figure 10-13**). The deviation from the true path is recorded as the machine is driven in a circle at various speeds.

System Accuracy

The precision plasma system can produce accurate results at thicknesses up to ½ inch (see **Figure 10-14**).

CAM Integration

Since computers are now used so often in designing parts, direct links to the CAM system should be used for part preparation. This can eliminate manual data entry and possible errors.

Computers are also efficient in keeping track of production requirements and job scheduling. Ultimately, though, the most important benefit is in the cutting pro-

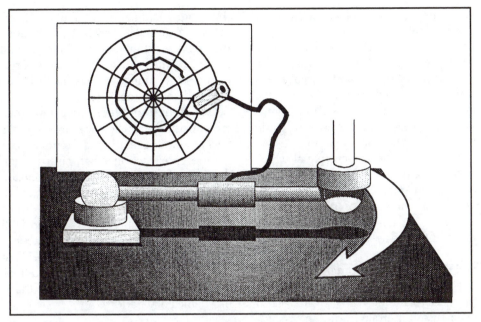

Figure 10-13. The ball bar test is used to determine how a machine will perform under cutting conditions.

cess calculation and the control of cutting conditions.

The precision plasma process is robust. This means it will tolerate wide variation in many parameters, eliminating the need for constant tuning by the operator.

The CAM control system can monitor and control cutting conditions. Using simple preliminary instructions given by the operator, it is possible to obtain the same high quality for all parts in a 100-part run or for a single part which is cut only once.

Case Studies

Electrical Panel and Cabinet Manufacturer. A control system manufacturer needed an efficient way to produce custom-designed electrical panels and cabinets in small quantities. Changing the standard welded design to bolt together

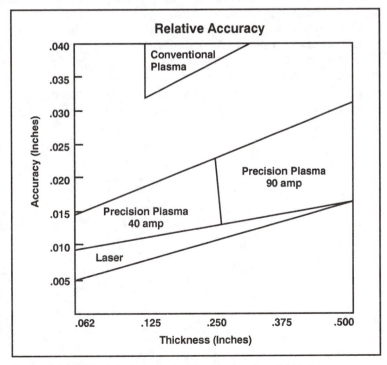

Figure 10-14. This chart compares the accuracy of precision plasma, conventional plasma, and laser.

versions reduced fixturing and welding but required cutting more complicated shapes.

The precision plasma system provided benefits in this use. For example, two control panels fabricated out of ³⁄₁₆-inch mild steel would usually take 45 minutes to shear, punch, and notch using the manufacturer's conventional process. With precision plasma cutting, those two panels were cut in eight minutes, including handling time.

In another example, a single-cut panel which consisted of three sections would have taken two workers two hours using the conventional means. It took 15 minutes with the precision plasma system. The manufacturer was able to reduce the turnaround time for custom enclosure fabrication to one day.

Commercial Laundry Equipment Manufacturer. A manufacturer of commercial laundry machines purchased its frame parts precut, and it needed to decrease turnaround time and reduce inventory. Half of this work is in ³⁄₁₆-inch thick material, and the variety required too much special tooling for a punch press.

After installing a precision plasma system, the actual cost of the parts was dramatically reduced, even when shipping and handling was included. However, a second unforeseen benefit provided an equally dramatic payback. The variety of individual assemblies had required extensive welding fixturing. Making use of the precision plasma accuracies and the flexibility of computer design, the manufacturer added a "mortis and tenon" feature to many of its parts. The parts are now nearly self-fixturing, and overall welding time has dropped considerably.

Construction Machinery Fabricator. Precision plasma technology can be used in a cell configuration with a punch and a forming press.

One construction machinery fabricator produces the floor pan of a small excavator in three steps. First, reference and small bolt holes are punched on a ¼-inch blank (approximately 3 feet by 4 feet). Next, the part is moved to the precision plasma table where larger cutouts, notches, and other edge details are added. The blank is then formed to produce the finished floor pan.

Each machine does the part of the job it can most efficiently perform.

Conclusion

High-quality, accurate, and dross-free parts may be cut from sheet metal and light plate when the precision plasma process is combined with appropriate machine systems. The data presented in chart form has been compiled from actual experience and fairly represents the results that can be expected with this technology.

How to evaluate CNCs
for thermal cutting:
Design features and comparisons

The popularity and practicality of thermal cutting controls skyrocketed with the advent of the microprocessor in the early 1970s. This technological breakthrough signaled the decline of optical tracing machines for metal fabrication and paved the way for today's most productive shape cutting methods.

With today's microprocessor-based computer numerical controls (CNCs), metal fabricators and suppliers are offered a variety of new capabilities that increase production capacity, reduce scrap losses, and improve cut quality.

CNC Advantages

Microprocessor-based CNCs revolutionized the flame cutting industry because they offered users immediate advantages.

Closer tolerances are possible. This advantage is important for fabricating large shapes and for cutting shapes that must be fit and welded together. By eliminating templates, setup is faster. Higher quality repeatability is possible because operators rely on a computer program instead of having to follow a template manually. Also, CNCs allow operators to chain cut easily. With one pierce, operators can continuously cut from row to row — difficult with a manual tracer. With CNCs, common side cutting, or cutting the sides of several parts at one

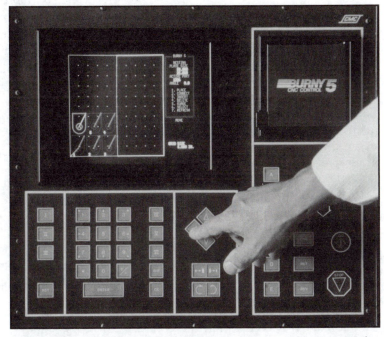

Before shape cutting with a CNC, an operator can view a graphic representation of the part program, as well as a comprehensive profile for both the part program and machine status.

time, is possible. This function was almost impossible with a tracer.

There are other productivity advantages. CNCs enable the machine to traverse from part to part automatically and rapidly. This eliminates the need to reposition the template table manually. Also, with canned shapes and manual data input (MDI) capabilities, there is no need to make templates for simple shapes. This can often result in cost savings. Consistent and precise cuts also enable operators to reduce scrap by programming in less wasted material and doing the job right the first time.

When should an optical tracer be maintained? When the expense of a CNC cannot be justified because a company does not cut that many parts or it does not need the accuracy the CNC can provide.

Basic Design Features

Most of today's microprocessor-based shape cutting controls have certain design features in common. Basic design features include:

1. **Membrane keyboard.** Most shape cutting controls face harsh environments. Sealed membrane keyboards keep dust, dirt, and contaminants out.

2. **RAM memory (with nonvolatile battery backup).** Operators can load and store part programs, use the program to cut shapes, and then delete the program or return it back to storage. These programs will be retained in the event of a power failure.

3. **Information display.** With vacuum phosphorous or liquid crystal display, operators always have immediate access to precise information. Today's most sophisticated units even use cathode ray tube (CRT) screens with high-resolution color graphics. These units provide a complete visual display of all cutting facts.

4. **Executive routine (stored on EPROM).** All information needed to run the control is in permanent storage. Older units had to be loaded with large spools of tape if the executive routine was lost.

5. **Auxiliary outputs.** Modern CNCs provide outputs for plate marking and for use with a programmable logic controller (PLC). With these systems, operators can also automatically control torch up-down, torch ignition, and gases on-off, etc.

6. **Menu-driven operation.** To facilitate use, most CNCs are menu-driven with some form of operator prompting.

7. **Diagnostics.** Almost any CNC offers some

method of diagnosing control problems should they occur.

Also, most CNCs for shape cutting offer built-in noise immunity features. These are important with plasma cutting machines.

Input and Programming

Today's CNCs for shape cutting offer an operator a variety of program input choices:

1. **Canned shapes.** Most CNCs offer some type of shape library (circles, rings, rectangles, etc.) for fast operator setup.

2. **MDI.** All CNCs provide operators some method of inputting their own custom shapes (XY coordinates) through the front control panel.

3. **Template teach.** Operators can teach most CNCs new shapes by tracing a template with a photo optical tracer.

4. **Serial communication direct numerical control (DNC).** Many controls enable the operator to communicate with an off-line programming center, host computer, computer-aided design (CAD) system, etc., for program loading and storage.

5. **Floppy disc.** Most CNC controls allow users the option of creating programs off-line with a personal computer (PC), copying onto a floppy disc, loading it into a floppy disc reader, and finally entering the program into the control for actual cutting.

6. **Paper tape.** Although this input method is becoming less popular, most CNCs still offer users the option of loading programs by way of punched tape.

Make sure your shape cutting CNC is compatible with these popular programming formats.

Any CNC available should be compatible with Word Address. This format for loading programs is generally considered to be the industry standard.

Most controls allow users the option of generating their own variable dimension custom shapes by a generic language, common to that specific control.

History of CNCs

This is one of first shape cutting controls, with a built-in paper tape.

requirements of shipbuilders, using tracing templates with ratios as big as 100:1, necessitated the first numerical control (NC). Using punched tape to accept programs, these controls configured the cutting process, especially for XY coordinate cutting. Unfortunately, early NCs were bulky, and they generated too much heat. Many even had to be housed in a separate air-conditioned room.

With the development of the microprocessor, the CNC for shape cutting was born. CNCs could be housed in a smaller box and mounted directly on the machine, and they offered fabricators a myriad of new shape cutting capabilities.

One of the first controls offered five standard shapes, had a limited memory — blocks back then, instead of bytes — and offered a form of manual programming. Punched tape input for complex shapes was also available.

Today, a variety of retrofit products and services to the flame cutting industry are available, as well as a range of shape cutting CNCs. This includes CNCs with built-in standard shape libraries, CNCs for high-production cutting that offer more memory and cartridge access, DNCs with built-in drive amplifier systems, and CNCs for maximum shape cutting capability.

These top-of-the-line CNCs offer maximum memory storage, color CRT screens for high-resolution graphic display, some form of on-screen part nesting, and may even include multitasking.

Although the oxyfuel process of cutting originated sometime around 1900, it was not adapted for mechanized cutting until the early 1950s. These cutting machines were known as traction-drive tracers because they actually used a traction-stylus to follow the template as the machine cut.

The photo optical tracer, invented in the 1960s, along with the introduction of the coordinate drive, improved the system to a degree. The large part

Although the ESSI format was more common to NCs and earlier CNCs, most controls are still compatible to ESSI.

Standard Run/Operational Features

As with any CNC, shape cutting controls continue to become more sophisticated each year with the addition of new features. The following operational features should be common to any controls under evaluation:

1. **Autocut mode.** This capability automates the cutting process by controlling preheat, torch on-off, etc. Operators can also switch to manual operation if needed.

2. **Pierce ramp.** This function, for thicker plate, allows the operator to achieve a more accurate pierce and reduce splatter by allowing the torch to creep into the plate.

3. **Return to pierce point (or home point).** This is the automatic return of the torch to the starting point at the press of a button.

4. **Return to cutter path.** This allows an operator to move torches into a location so they can be serviced, with an automatic return to the cutting path.

5. **Backup (for lost cut recovery).** Operators can automatically back up a torch on path. This is important with multiple torches, should one fail.

6. **Test run feature.** This allows the shape program to be test run and allows the operator to shift the program over the material. This is important when using remnants.

7. **Corner slowdown.** This automatically slows a torch down and freezes height control as it enters a corner, which is important for high-speed plasma cutting.

8. **Auto advance to next part.** As discussed before, CNCs allow the machine to rapidly traverse to the next part.

9. **Status displays.** All CNCs provide the operator with some form of status display to monitor the speed of the machine, the number of parts cut, and numerous other cutting processes.

10. **Geometric functions.** All shape cutting CNCs should offer some type of kerf compensation, part rotation, mirror imaging of shapes, scaling (up or down) of parts, and automatic plate alignment. This relatively new function automatically aligns a misaligned plate parallel to the machine rails so it will follow the part program and then can be cut.

Comparing Different Controls

Although many of today's shape cutting CNCs offer similar features and capabilities, there are still major differences to consider.

For instance, how user-friendly is the control? All the features in the world mean little if it is difficult to use. This point takes on added significance for first-time shape cutting control users.

What are production requirements? A variety of shape cutting controls are available in a range of prices. Make certain the features and capabilities of the control satisfy immediate needs.

Along with this concern, make sure the CNC is expandable. If production requirements should change in the future, will the control adapt? Will the company be able to add on to the system?

Then, take a close look inside the shape cutting control. Will it be easy to service? Is it modular so that a company can usually service the control itself? What type of service program does the manufacturer offer? Does it offer a loaner program should the unit fail?

Finally, along with the control, take a closer look at the manufacturing source. Is it a shape cutting CNC manufacturer that offers a specially-designed shape cutting control? Or is it a control manufacturer that also offers a general-purpose control adapted for shape cutting? There is a big difference.

Also, what type of sales and service facility does the manufacturer maintain? What type of personnel does it offer? Is the staff knowledgeable about oxyfuel and plasma cutting, and are they responsible to individual needs?

Shape Cutting Trends

Along with operator prompting in foreign languages, the newest trends in shape cutting include the color CRT screen with high-resolution graphics and multitasking, which is the ability to perform more than one task at one time.

Are these functions necessary? It depends on the sophistication of a system, how much capability is needed, and how important it is to have complete visual access to all cutting facts at all times.

What does the future of shape cutting CNCs hold in store? To some degree, control technology is only limited by the imagination. More specifically, metal fabricators can probably count on more memory in a smaller box, even more multitasking capabilities, and the advent of totally automated shape cutting systems.

Cost estimating and economics of thermal cutting:
A down-to-earth look at plasma arc and oxyfuel cutting costs

Over the years, numerous methods have been used to determine the costs attributed to thermal cutting. Cost comparisons developed by product suppliers clearly illustrate their cost advantages.

Fabricators generally arrive at their costs after the fact, then project these to determine future anticipated costs. Manufacturers conduct in-house cost comparisons based on historical data combined with anticipated improvements associated with changes in cost-affecting areas.

Regardless of the method used, the findings are usually accurate because they are based on a specific set of conditions. The model has been neatly qualified and will produce accurate results when all of the "if" qualifiers have been satisfied.

Note that "if qualifiers" simply means that "if" a particular condition exists, "then" the result will reflect the condition. For example, "if" plasma arc were used to cut ½-inch thick carbon steel plate, "then" the cut time would be less than "if" oxyfuel were used. General statements are never accurately made without "if" qualifiers.

The "if" qualifying variables required to determine thermal cutting costs include:

1. Operating equipment available.
    * Numerical control
    * Photo tracer control
    * Machine speed range and performance capabilities
2. Cutting process available.
    * Oxyfuel
    * Plasma arc
3. Number of cutting heads simultaneously available per process.
4. Maximum machine availability.
5. Operating and material handling personnel available.
6. Cutting head minimum spacing and maximum travel.
7. Part programming/template preparation equipment available.
8. Material available.
    * Grade
    * Chemistry
    * Length
    * Width
    * Thickness
    * Number of plates
9. Material handling capabilities.
    * Magnet
    * Vacuum lift
    * Crane hooks
    * Number of cutting tables
    * Programmable conveyor system
10. Parts to cut.
    * Quantity
    * Length and width for separation
    * Area per part
    * Number of inside cutouts per part
    * Total linear inches of cut per part

11. Fuel gas type for oxyfuel.

12. Power available for plasma arc.

13. Cost per foot of cut or per part.
    * Fuel gas
    * Oxygen
    * Nitrogen
    * Argon and hydrogen
    * Electricity
    * Oxyfuel torch consumables
    * Plasma arc consumables
    * Direct labor — machine operator.
    * Direct labor — material handler.
    * Direct labor — programmer or
      template maker
    * Incremental overhead
    * Incremental overhead — material handler
    * Incremental overhead — programmer or
      template maker
    * Equipment maintenance
    * Miscellaneous expenses—torches,
      cutting table slats, etc.
    * Material

14. Torch-on time duty cycle.

15. Material utilization.

16. Material handling efficiency.

17. Scrap parts.

The variables associated with cost estimating will produce an infinite number of possible combinations.

Effect of Variables

The net effect of the variables can be divided into three categories:

1. Consumables required for part quantity

2. Programming or template preparation time required per part, regardless of quantity

3. Per-hour operating costs

Consumables include all gases, torch tip parts, and, in the case of plasma arc, electricity.

Once established, programming or template preparation costs may be prorated over total parts required. After they are accounted for, subsequent runs could eliminate this one-time cost.

Per-hour operating costs will dramatically affect the per-part cost. These include incremental overhead, direct labor, prorated maintenance and miscellaneous expenses, and equipment power usage.

Examples of Variable Influences

If a choice may be made in favor of using plasma arc over oxyfuel or multiple torch operation over single torch operation, these will show the most dramatic effect on the per-part cost because of reduced cutting time.

If the material can be cut using the oxyfuel process, then the alloy content will affect the cutting speed. This may have a significant effect on per-part cost. For example, if 1-inch-thick AISI 1020 material could be oxyfuel cut at 18 inches per minute (IPM), then 1-inch-thick AISI 4340 would be cut at a reduced rate because of the inhibiting characteristics of the alloys on the chemical reaction between iron and cutting oxygen.

If a fabricator believes that one particular fuel gas can offer an increased cutting speed over a different fuel gas and the gas costs do not offset the speed advantage, then this may have a marginal effect on the per-part cost. For example, acetylene offers a more concentrated, localized primary preheating zone than natural gas and, therefore, requires less preheating time to elevate carbon steel to its kindling temperature. Additionally, a hotter primary flame will elevate the plate temperature faster than a wide-area preheating fuel gas, therefore suggesting a higher cutting speed.

To illustrate the cost allocations, the model shown in **Figure 11-1** will be used.

Based on typical cutting speeds, consumable life, gas consumption, material handling capabilities, and power requirements, **Figure 11-2** illustrates the cost distribution effect of the various possible torch combinations.

The consumables required per foot of cut remain constant whether one torch or multiple torches are used to complete the cutting requirement. The use of multiple torches reduces the time it takes to complete the cutting requirements and, therefore, reduces the per-hour operating costs.

The process selection — oxyfuel versus plasma arc — will affect the per-hour operating cost because cutting speeds are different. The consumables required also change with the process, offering a different per foot of cut base. Both processes, however, maintain a constant "consumables required per foot of cut" regardless of the number of multiple torches used.

The remaining variable is the cost associated with the preparation of the numerical control (NC) part program for a specific part or group of parts. This is a one-time cost and will be distributed over the quantity of parts required. If the part geometry is unique and only one piece is required, then the entire cost of preparing the NC part program will be reflected in the cost-per-piece part. These "one-of-a-kind" piece parts may, therefore, be considerably more expensive to process than multiple parts.

The Role of Material Handling

The common denominator for "per-hour operating cost" is combined cutting speed. By increasing the number of cutting heads simultaneously used, and/or selecting a faster cutting process, the per-piece part cost will be reduced.

This will not result in a linear cost reduction, however, because of material handling considerations. There will be a combined cutting speed at which one person will be unable to remove cut piece parts as fast as the machine can cut them. This would typically occur around 80 IPM combined cutting speed.

At this point, the machine torch-on time will be reduced, or an assistant will be required to help load plate and unload cut parts. The arrival of the material handling assistant will relieve the machine

Material	
Grade	AISI 1,020 Hours
Thickness	1 Inch
Plate Size	84 x 240 Inches
Piece Part	
Quantity Required	50 Each
Width for Torch Spacing	12.5 Inches
Length for Repeat Rows	24.5 Inches
Number of Inside Cutouts/Part	1 Each
Combined Linear Inches Cut/Part	80 Inches
Time Required to Make NC Program	
(On a Per-Piece Basis)	.5 Hour
Equipment	
CNC Thermal Machining Center	
Number of Oxyfuel Torches	6
Number of Plasma Arc Torches	6
Fuel Gas Used (Oxyfuel)	Natural Gas
Plasma Arc Type – Water Injected, Nitrogen Gas	600 Amps
Personnel Available	
Machine Operator	1
Material Handler	1
Programmer	1
Consumable Costs	
Oxyfuel Torch Tip	$ 11.50
Plasma Arc Electrode	$ 22.00
Plasma Arc Nozzle	$ 22.00
Natural Gas/100 Cubic Feet	$ .64
Oxygen/100 Cubic Feet	$ 1.00
Nitrogen/100 Cubic Feet	$ 1.00
Electric Power/KWH	$ .78
Personnel Costs	
Direct Labor for Operator	$ 9.35
Direct Labor for Material Handler	$ 8.15
Direct Labor for Programmer	$ 9.75
Incremental Overhead:	
Operator and Machine	$ 25.00
Material Handler	$ 8.00
General Expenses	
Machine Maintenance/Hour	$ 3.00
(Based on 1 Shift Operation at 50% Torch-on Time)	
Miscellaneous Expenses/Hour	$ 2.00
(e.g., Torches, Cutting Table, Slat Replacement, etc.)	

Figure 11-1. This is a model to illustrate cost allocation for determining the effects of variables.

operator of responsibilities which had kept the torch-on time potential at a reduced level.

It is reasonable to expect a higher torch-on time with both the machine operator and the material handler working together. In fact, the increased torch-on time should more than offset the increased labor costs.

As fabricators continue to increase the combined cutting speed, they will eventually reach a

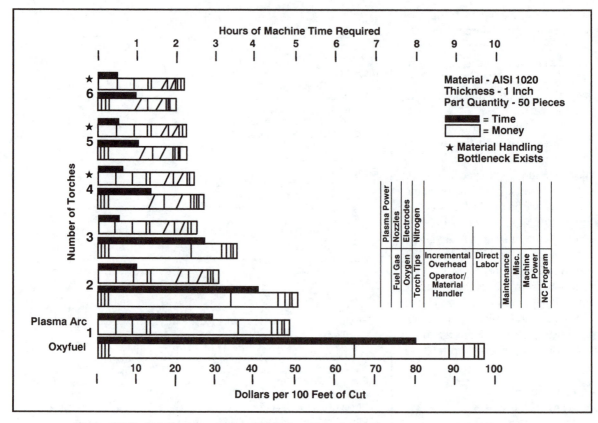

Figure 11-2. This illustrates the cost distribution effect of the various possible torch combinations.

point at which parts again cannot be offloaded and plates reloaded onto the cutting tables fast enough to keep up with the cutting machine.

This point would typically occur at around 180 IPM combined cutting speed. At this increased combined cutting speed, the machine torch-on time will likely be reduced.

Adding more people to assist in the material handling efforts will have little effect unless additional cutting tables are available, complete with material handling equipment. The material handling bottleneck must be addressed to expect improved throughput capabilities as the combined cutting speed crosses this threshold.

Consumable Costs

As the "per-hour operating cost" is reduced by increased combined cutting speed, the consumable costs become more apparent.

The bill for consumables will normally be higher for the plasma arc process than for the oxyfuel process. As the material thickness increases, the power required for the plasma arc process increases. As the arc current increases, the life expectancy of the consumable hardware decreases.

If the material can be cut using either oxyfuel or plasma arc, as in the model shown in Figure 11-2, then the consumable cost for part quantity will usually be two to five times as much using plasma arc as oxyfuel.

Because of this, the magnitude of cost reductions associated with the reduction in per-hour operating costs resulting from increasing the number of cutting heads will be less apparent for plasma arc than oxyfuel. This becomes more noticeable as the arc current increases as the material thickness increases.

Comparing Possibilities

The cost per 100 feet of cut based on Figure 11-2 gives an advantage to four oxyfuel torches at $26.92 per 100 feet, as opposed to two plasma arc torches at $30.87 per 100 feet (see **Figure 11-3**). However, the scheduled machine time for the production run favors plasma arc at 1 hour over oxyfuel at 1 hour, 21 minutes, and 18 seconds.

If machine capacity presents a problem, the decision would likely be to sacrifice the per-part cost in favor of the increased throughput capability. Note that a one-torch cost comparison gives plasma arc a two-to-one advantage.

By altering one or more of a seemingly infinite number of variable combinations, the economic advantages which appear obvious may become elusive. An example is illustrated in **Figure 11-4**. Here, the only change from the model in Figure 11-2 is material thickness. The ½-inch-thick material can be cut using the plasma arc process at a much higher feed rate than 1-inch-thick material (105 IPM versus 50 IPM). The difference in oxyfuel cutting speed is only 22 IPM versus 18 IPM.

Additional advantages include reduced arc current and increased nozzle and electrode life.

Plasma Arc						
Number of Torches Used	**1**	**2**	**3**	**4**	**5**	**6**
*Plasma Power	$ 4.35	$ 4.35	$ 4.35	$ 4.35	$ 4.35	$ 4.35
*Nozzles	3.96	3.96	3.96	3.96	3.96	3.96
*Electrode	3.96	3.96	3.96	3.96	3.96	3.96
*Nitrogen	.75	.75	.75	.75	.75	.75
*Incremental Overhead						
Operator and Machine	22.50	7.50	5.00	4.69	3.75	3.13
Material Handler	——	2.40	1.60	1.50	1.20	1.00
*Direct Labor						
Operator	8.42	2.81	1.87	1.75	1.40	1.17
Material Handler	——	2.45	1.63	1.53	1.22	1.02
*Maintenance	1.35	.68	.45	.34	.27	.23
*Miscellaneous	.90	.45	.30	.23	.18	.15
*Machine Power	.35	.12	.08	.07	.06	.05
NC Program	4.88	4.88	4.88	4.88	4.88	4.88
Processing Costs/ 100 Feet of Cut	48.00	30.87	25.41	24.59	22.57	21.22
Material Cost/Part	26.03	26.03	26.03	26.03	26.03	26.03
Processing Cost/Part	3.20	2.06	1.69	1.64	1.50	1.41
Scheduled Machine Time (Hours)	3.00	1.00	.67	.63	.50	.42
Oxyfuel						
Number of Torches Used	**1**	**2**	**3**	**4**	**5**	**6**
*Fuel Gas	$ .23	$ .23	$ .23	$ .23	$ .23	$ .23
*Oxygen	2.32	2.32	2.32	2.32	2.32	2.32
*Torch Tips	.70	.70	.70	.70	.70	.70
*Incremental Overhead						
Operator and Machine	60.97	30.49	20.32	10.16	8.13	6.77
Material Handler	——	——	——	3.25	2.60	2.17
*Direct Labor						
Operator	22.80	11.40	7.60	3.80	3.04	2.53
Material Handler	——	——	——	3.31	2.65	2.21
*Maintenance	3.66	1.83	1.22	.91	.73	.61
*Miscellaneous	2.44	1.22	.81	.61	.49	.41
*Machine Power	.95	.48	.32	.16	.13	.11
NC Program	4.88	4.88	4.88	4.88	4.88	4.88
Processing Cost/ 100 Feet of Cut	95.54	50.13	34.99	26.92	22.48	19.52
Material Cost/Part	26.03	26.03	26.03	26.03	26.03	26.03
Processing Cost/Part	6.37	3.34	2.33	1.79	1.50	1.30
Scheduled Machine Time (Hours)	8.13	4.06	2.71	1.35	1.08	.90

*Cost per 100 feet of cut.

Figure 11-3. The cost breakdown for torch multiples one through six, based on the model conditions shown in Figure 11-1, is shown here.

The possible disadvantage lies in the increased commitment to material handling. A bottleneck may occur as soon as two plasma arc torches are used to simultaneously cut parts.

The cost per 100 feet of cut, based on Figure 11-4, gives a cost advantage to six oxyfuel torches at $15.32 over two plasma arc torches at

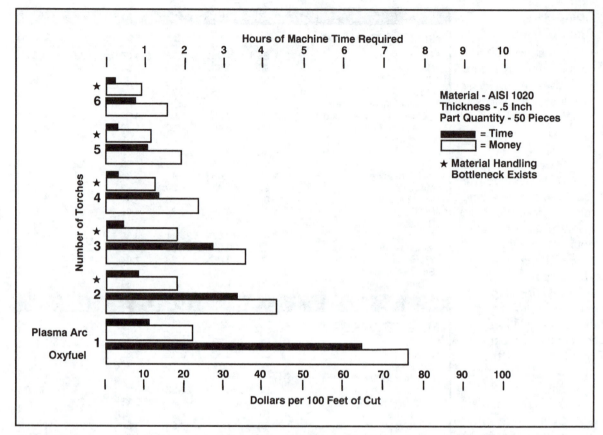

Figure 11-4. By altering one or more of the variable combinations, apparent economic advantages may become elusive. In this chart, the only change from the model in Figure 11-2 is material thickness.

$16.00. However, the scheduled machine time for the production run favors plasma arc at 40 minutes over oxyfuel at 44 minutes. Note that a one-torch cost comparison gives plasma arc a 3.4-to-1 advantage over oxyfuel.

Cost Estimating

The formulas shown in **Figures 11-5** and **11-6** illustrate the variables which must be analyzed to determine production costs accurately. Considering the number of calculations required for each different "model," it is not surprising that cost estimating of thermal cutting has been done empirically.

The introduction of the computer to manufacturing offers high-speed processing of "model"

conditions. Decisions regarding scheduling, routing, inventories, processing times, material utilization, purchasing, fuel gas selection, process selection, machinery, etc., can all be by-products of economic comparison.

The proliferation of computers and application software offer quick and convenient analysis of operating variables.

Conclusion

Any general statements will only apply to a specific set of "if" qualifiers. A detailed analysis of specific "models" will be required to determine accurately the economics and estimated costs associated with thermal cutting.

Formula for Cost Estimating – Oxyfuel

Torch-on Time = (Linear Feet of Cut/Cutting Speed in Inches per Hour + Rapid Traverse Time + (Preheat Time/Piece x Number of Pierces)

Duty Cycle = Torch-on Time/Machine Time Required

Note: Figure the Following Costs for the Entire Production Run of Parts

+ Torch Tip Cost = (Dollars/Tip/Life Expectancy in Hours)/Torch-on Time in Hours + (Dollars/Tip/200 x Number of Pierces)

+ Oxygen Cost = (Consumption [cfh] x Torch-on Time [Hours]) x Dollars/Cubic Foot

+ Fuel Gas Cost = (Consumption [cfh] x Torch-on Time [Hours]) x Dollars/Cubic Foot

+ Operator Incremental Overhead = Overhead Rate per Hour x (Torch-on Time [Hours]/Duty Cycle)

+ Material Handler Incremental Overhead = Overhead Rate per Hour x (Torch-on Time [Hours]/Duty Cycle)

+ Cutting Machine Incremental Overhead = Overhead Rate per Hour x (Torch-on Time [Hours]/Duty Cycle)

+ Operator Direct Labor = Wages (Dollars/Hour) x (Torch-on Time [Hours]/Duty Cycle)

+ Material Handler Direct Labor = Wages (Dollars/Hour) x (Torch-on Time [Hours]/Duty Cycle)

+ General Maintenance Expenses = (Annual Maintenance Cost [Dollars]/Operating Hours Available) x (Torch-on Time/Duty Cycle)

+ General Miscellaneous Expenses = (Annual Cost for Torches + Cutting Table Slats + Raw Stock Handling + Inventory Tax, etc.)/(Operating Hours Available) x (Torch-on Time/Duty Cycle)

+ Machine Power = Dollars/Kilowatt Hour x (Torch-on Time/Duty Cycle) x 5 Kilowatts

+ NC Programming = Time to Prepare Part Program (Hours) x (Programmer Hourly Wage + Incremental Overhead Hourly Rate)

= Total Processing Cost (Note: Add Raw Material Cost for Total Cost)

Figure 11-5.

Formula for Cost Estimating – Plasma Arc

Torch-on Time = (Linear Feet of Cut/Cutting Speed in Inches per Hour + Rapid Traverse Time + (Preheat Time/Piece x Number of Pierces)

Duty Cycle = Torch-on Time/Machine Time Required

Note: Figure the Following Costs for the Entire Production Run of Parts

+ Nozzle Cost = (Dollars/Nozzle/Life Expectancy in Hours)/Torch-on Time in Hours + (Dollars/Nozzle/200 x Number of Pierces)

+ Electrode Cost = (Dollars/Electrode/Life Expectancy in Hours)/Torch-on Time in Hours

+ Nitrogen Cost = (Consumption [cfh] x Torch-on Time [Hours]) x Dollars/Cubic Foot

+ Operator Incremental Overhead = Overhead Rate per Hour x (Torch-on Time [Hours]/Duty Cycle)

+ Material Handler Incremental Overhead = Overhead Rate per Hour x (Torch-on Time [Hours]/Duty Cycle)

+ Cutting Machine Incremental Overhead = Overhead Rate per Hour x (Torch-on Time [Hours]/Duty Cycle)

+ Operator Direct Labor = Wages (Dollars/Hour) x (Torch-on Time [Hours]/Duty Cycle)

+ Material Handler Direct Labor = Wages (Dollars/Hour) x (Torch-on Time [Hours]/Duty Cycle)

+ General Maintenance Expenses = (Annual Maintenance Cost [Dollars]/Operating Hours Available) x (Torch-on Time/Duty Cycle)

+ General Miscellaneous Expenses = (Annual Cost for Torches + Cutting Table Slats + Raw Stock Handling + Inventory Tax, etc.)/(Operating Hours Available) x (Torch-on Time/Duty Cycle)

+ Machine Power = Dollars/Kilowatt Hour x (Torch-on Time/Duty Cycle x 5 Kilowatts + [Dollars/Kilowatt Hour x Torch-on Time]) x (Operating Current x Voltage/1,000/.8 [Power Factor Correction])

+ NC Programming = Time to Prepare Part Program (Hours) x (Programmer Hourly Wage + Incremental Overhead Hourly Rate)

= Total Processing Cost (Note: Add Raw Material Cost for Total Cost)

Figure 11-6.

Cutting steel for quality and safety

In much the same manner that microwave ovens have found their way into kitchens — not to replace conventional ovens, but to use when time and ease of use are critical — ultrathermic cutting can be a complement to traditional oxyacetylene and carbon arc outfits.

Ultrathermics can often assist specialty metal fabrication and heavy equipment repair operations. While this type of cutting will never relegate oxyacetylene or carbon arc rigs to the far corners of the shop, it can help fabricators attain speed in cutting or gouging a range of materials.

Such systems can be used for quick cutting, piercing, or gouging of many materials, including those that oxyacetylene cannot cut,

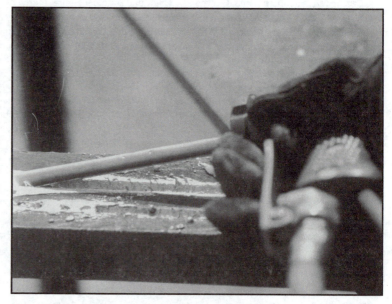

Figure 12-1. Gouging with ultrathermic technology leaves no carbon deposits.

pierce, or gouge. The process has been used to cut materials such as aluminum, titanium, stainless steel, brass, and cast iron. It can also cut steel more than 6 inches thick. Concrete, refractory materials, and copper can be pierced.

The equipment can be used for quickly gouging cracks or old welds, since the work surface does not need to be cleaned or ground before laying down the new welds.

Comparison to Traditional Methods

Gouging can be performed with the system's equipment (see **Figure 12-1**). Unlike air-carbon arc, however, the systems do not require welding machines or air compressors, which helps create a safe, clean work environment.

Ancillary equipment is also eliminated. There is no carbon buildup, which means no grinding or gouge cleaning before welding.

The cutting systems differ from traditional oxyacetylene counterparts in a number of ways. Both are flame processes using oxygen as a fuel. However, oxyacetylene burns at approximately 5,800 degrees Fahrenheit using acetylene as a secondary fuel. Setup can be lengthy, involving two regulators, two sets of hoses, and a variable torch. Preheating is required before any cutting can take place.

Ultrathermic systems use oxygen and consumable steel and alloy fuel rods. No hazardous secondary fuels are used.

System Components

A basic system is comprised of the hand-held torch, ultrathermic rods, a striker plate for generating an ignition arc, an oxygen supply with regulator, and a 12-volt direct current (DC) battery. Ignited by an electric spark, the rods burn at temperatures of more than 10,000 degrees Fahrenheit. Because the system operates at such high temperature, the target material liquifies almost instantly, and preheating is not required.

This cutting process is a derivative of oxyarc cutting. In oxyarc, an arc is struck between an electrode and the metal to be cut. A molten puddle is formed as a result of that arc. Oxygen, introduced through a hollow electrode, increases the temperature of the puddle. In addition to the rapid melting, the pressure of the gas jet drives the molten metal away, forming the cut (see **Figure 12-2**).

The ultrathermic cutting process differs from oxyarc in that once an arc is struck, the ultrathermic rod will continue to burn without maintaining an electric current. The rod acts as a thermic lance. The arc is only required to ignite the rod. Rapid oxidation occurs at the point of contact between the arc and the alloy wires within the rods. This chemical reaction heats the wires to their respective kindling points. The temperature attained by the burning rod is much higher than the melting point of the target work material. The rod will continue to burn only for as long as oxygen is supplied, or until the rod is consumed.

Applications

One of the most common applications of the systems in repairing heavy equipment is the removal of frozen or mushroomed pins. A pin

Figure 12-2. Cutting of 1-inch steel is shown here. The rod tip in the cut prevents blowback while increasing cutting efficiency.

freezes up because excess grinding wear causes it to become imbedded in the bore. Mushrooming occurs when the pin gives way from stress or impact.

The removal of a worn or damaged pin can be both time-consuming and costly. Not only are expenses involved in the actual removal, but also indirectly through down equipment.

Using ultrathermics, a 6-inch track pin can be removed and replaced in less than one hour. In most cases, a frozen pin can be replaced in about 20 minutes, while a mushroomed pin usually takes 30 to 40 minutes. The technique involves piercing the length of the pin and then quenching it with water. This causes the pin to shrink in diameter, allowing it to be easily pressed out. Repeating the piercing process facilitates the removal of the most stubborn pins.

Plant maintenance applications involving piercing are setting of machinery anchor bolts, removing frozen bolts and nuts, and boring through concrete for pipe and conduit installation. Fabricators can use the systems for piercing starter holes for plasma cutting of thick materials.

A new emphasis is being placed on alternative methods of gouging both steel and exotic materials. Plasma arc is gaining in popularity because, like ultrathermics, it is both clean and quick. However, compact ultrathermic equipment is portable and lends itself to field repair because it does not need compressed air (or exotic gas) and electricity.

When the systems are used for repairs of cracks and stress fractures, weld preparation is minimized. Resultant slag from the gouge is easily chipped away.

Since the base material is not contaminated by carbon or any other matter, the material is ready to accept the new weld. The system's gouging capabilities are also an expedient means of removing existing welds and hardfacing.

Not a cure-all for every repair or maintenance situation, ultrathermics can expand a technician's capabilities to perform applications that often cannot be done as efficiently using oxyacetylene or air-carbon arc.

Retrofitting older flame cutting machinery: An alternative to purchasing new equipment

According to industry reports, as many as 6,000 to 8,000 flame cutting machines are currently in use in the U.S. that are at least 10 years old. These machines often represent the fabrication lifeblood for manufacturers, and for good reason.

All production typically starts there. Subsequent fabrication and machining operations rely on flame-cut metal shapes so they can take the next steps. For exact part fit-up and assembly, these machines must be capable of flame cutting each shape to consistent quality standards and to exact specifications.

Today, many of these manufacturers are facing the same set of problems. As machinery ages, it tends to deteriorate and break down. Plus, dramatic advances in control technology have evolved in just the last several years. Computerization is already multiplying yesterday's productivity limitations, aging (and dating) those same machines even more.

Each year, more manufacturers and fabricators are wrestling with the same question. Should we retrofit and rebuild our existing machine, or do we purchase a new one? Based on industry knowledge and application experiences, many manufacturers should consider a retrofit. It is a viable alternative to buying new equipment.

A Brief History

Although the oxyfuel process of cutting originated sometime around the turn of the century, it was not adapted for mechanized cutting until the early 1950s. The first generation of cantilever machinery used the same basic XY coordinate design that still exists today.

On one side of the machine, flame cutting torches are cantilevered out over an unsupported rail and a fabricated steel table that supports the cutting activity.

On the other side of the operator, the machine supports some form of tracing operation. Magnetic tracers represented the first generation of tracing capability. Using a pantagraph, the machine magnetically followed the perimeter of a previously cut part. In that way, the torches could duplicate the part by cutting the same shape out of the metal plate on the other side of the operator.

The first optical tracing machines were known as traction-drive tracers because they actually used a traction-stylus to physically follow the template as the machine cut. Improvements to this system included a long axis roller drive which allowed the driving wheel to be moved from the template to a larger roller.

With the advent of numerical controls (NCs) and

coordinate drive tracers, the future of today's computerized cantilever machinery came into focus.

The requirements of shipbuilders helped necessitate the first large gantry flame cutting machines. With this XY coordinate machine style, both ends of the cutting beam are supported over the large cutting area. Often, two sets of drives are required to moved the control and torches over the long axis.

For gantries, optical template tracing is routinely performed off-line. As recently as 10 years ago, it was also accomplished by ratio — as big as 100:1. Again, computerization and computer numerical control (CNC) technology would soon change that.

The basic mechanics of oxyfuel flame cutting have remained almost unchanged since it was mechanized in the 1950s. Plasma cutting, introduced in the 1960s, continued to evolve, offering fabricators more options every year for increased cutting speeds and cutting quality.

Still, the same basic technology required to move the torches, plasma, or oxyfuel remains unchanged. Most cantilever and gantry designs are still effective. Yesterday's structural steel frameworks are still functional.

In addition, new machinery is often too expensive for a fabricator's budgetary restraints. Also, it is sometimes difficult even to duplicate yesterday's craftsmanship.

Retrofitting older machinery is more than just an option. For many manufacturers, it is the answer. It can pay back the manufacturer more dividends than originally anticipated. The following case histories help illustrate this.

Smaller Cantilever Retrofit

Wain Roy, located near Worcester, Mass., has a 40-year history of manufacturing backhoes and buckets for heavy-duty machinery. Even though the company serves a niche market and has a few competitors, a tight economy has forced it to search hard for new ways to increase productivity.

Its 15-year-old flame cutting machine was an easy find. The small cantilever accommodated a 10-foot by 6-foot plate, used a single plasma torch, and cut at 30 inches per minute (IPM).

The company discovered numerous productivity shortcomings. Management calculated that the machine was averaging 55 percent scrap per plate (typical plate range from $\frac{3}{16}$ inch thick to 3 inches thick) by computing the weight of the finished product to the weight of the original raw material.

Management also discovered that during peak fabrication periods, the company was subcontracting out much of the work because of the capability limitations of the machine, hindering its productivity more. Because of budgetary limitations, new machinery was never a consideration.

After months of searching out and then reviewing various product alternatives, management decided on a retrofit. The company doubled the torch capacity and replaced the older control system with a CNC for integrated computer-aided design/computer-aided manufacturing (CAD/CAM) capabilities with the off-line programming center. Previously, CAD was used for template design only.

The CNC control package integrated a CNC with standard shapes, a 60-watt rack and pinion drive system, and a photo-optic tracing system capable of speeds up to 120 IPM. Only 60 to 80 IPM of tracing speed were required for plasma cutting. The company calculated that the system retrofit would pay for itself within six months.

As a result, automatic flame cutting, downloaded from the off-line center, and multiple torch capacity almost eliminated outside contracts at peak periods. Maximum plate utilization, from CNC-aided nesting, reduced previous scrap losses.

Surprisingly, the retrofit paid for itself within only three months. According to the vice president of manufacturing, one of its first jobs after the retrofit was cutting 100 units, and it saved the company $780. He said it did not take many of those jobs to pay off the investment.

Another smaller cantilever retrofit recently took place at the Everett Maintenance Shop for MBTA (Massachusetts Bay Transportation Authority).

The shop maintains 450 rapid transit cars, 200 light rail vehicles, 1,400 buses, and a mammoth system of support. The company is an integral part of that support system. It performs all repair and maintenance.

The company's 4½-foot by 6-foot oxyfuel flame machine was installed in 1974. It also used the old traction-style drive for photo-optic template tracing.

According to the truck shop supervisor, the optic eye was unreliable and constantly out of adjustment; even cleaning the glass table would throw it off. It was difficult to get an exact trace. The drive would slip around corners and lose the line, and finding parts for the old drive system was practically impossible.

Initially, only a new drive and tracer system retrofit was approved. During the retrofit process, the shop realized it could incorporate a CNC package that integrated a CNC control, a photo-optic tracing system, and a 60-watt rack and pinion drive system at about the same cost.

Before the new CNC package, all parts had to be traced to be cut. Now, more than 50 percent of all shapes are cut with the CNC's standard shape library. Parts that still need to be traced are quickly entered into the CNC with a template teach function.

Once entered, the operator tells the CNC how many parts to cut, allowing it to cut parts automatically. Also, because of the sensitivity and detail of the new drive and tracer system, the shop now cuts various parts that were previously bought elsewhere.

A flat metal probe with a somewhat unique shape, such as 7 inches long, 2 inches wide, and with three holes in it, was one of those parts. According to the truck shop supervisor, the company used to purchase these parts for $54 each; now it manufactures the part in-house for as little as $7.

Larger Cantilevers

The Gradall Company in New Philadelphia, Ohio, is an international manufacturer of excavators, rough-terrain forklifts, and special scalers. As with many manufacturers, all production starts (or

stops) with its flame cutting machine, a 1966 model with a template table of 48 inches by 100 inches.

Because of the heavy-duty nature of its product line, the company typically cuts prime plates of 80 inches by 240 inches and up to 10 inches thick.

Company management attributed the need for a retrofit to excessive repair costs of the control, downtime, and the inordinate cost of making, storing, and updating mylar templates. Because those problems could be corrected with a new control and drive system only, new machinery was never a consideration.

Downtime alone — from constant electrical problems — were costing the company more than $4,500 a year. Scrap and rework quality and technology shortcomings were costing more than $4,000 a year. Final approval to retrofit the cantilever was given after management calculated that the new CNC and 150-watt drive system retrofit would save the company approximately $19,800 a year.

The CNC, with 128K of expandable memory, provides automatic advance for high-production cutting. It accepts custom programs on cartridge or by floppy disk. It can also conduct two-way communications with an off-line center.

The company's retrofit included a file server software system. With this package, the company now designs parts in an off-line programming center, stores them, then downloads the programs at will through a direct numerical control (DNC) link to the CNC control mounted on the flame cutting machine.

Large Gantries

Large gantries offer big capabilities, often at a big expense. To combat this, many fabricators network, helping each other out with spare parts when their older machine goes down.

Such was the case in York, Pennsylvania. Before retrofitting, York International, an international manufacturer of large-scale refrigeration systems, and MPSI, an international manufacturer of mineral processing equipment for the mining industry, often kept in close contact.

Both companies relied heavily on their 10-year-old flame cutting machines to maintain production continuity, and both companies were experiencing downtime and cut quality shortcomings on a regular basis. When the control systems went down, it was a mad scramble to find replacement parts.

As the situations worsened, all options were considered. In both cases, new machinery was ruled out because both managers in charge came to the separate conclusion that they could retrofit their gantry with modern capabilities for somewhere between 10 and 20 percent of the cost of a new machine.

Both companies retrofitted their gantries with a CNC with graphic cathode ray tube (CRT) display, graphic part program nesting, and an ability to monitor the cutting function graphically as it takes place. MPSI also included a new drive system with 1,000 watts of power per axis, based on the recommendation of the retrofit specialist.

York International's retrofit included repositioning the large gantry, fixing several of the rails that had been damaged by forklifts, and converting the torches to 100 percent oxyfuel from partial plasma. Management approved the retrofit after they calculated a payback of less than two years.

With its code conversion feature, the CNC was able to convert and understand York's entire library of 20,000 to 30,000 part programs — an enormous expense if each program had to be relearned by the control.

The retrofit also helped York automate its system. Part programs can be downloaded to the CNC by two-way communications, and all other auxiliary functions of the oxyfuel machine can also be downloaded, including torch spacing, automatic torch height control, and automatic ignition.

MPSI's large gantry — 18 feet wide with two 30-foot-long water tables — routinely cuts 14½-foot plate with six oxyfuel torches and a plasma torch. Because of the CNC's graphic nesting and monitoring functions, the company was able to use more of each plate and minimize its scrap losses.

Programs are downloaded to the CNC from an off-line center, and operators can then nest and view each cutting operation, even under water. The company's manufacturing engineering manager said 92 to 93 percent of each plate is now being utilized.

MPSI's retrofit also included a new 1,000 watt rack and pinion drive system. Previously, its motors were taxed to full capacity. The new drive system provides power to spare, said the manufacturing engineering manager, providing precision, higher resolution for smoother edges, and better overall cutting accuracy.

He said that downtime problems have been eliminated. Also, by not purchasing a new machine, the company may have only lost overall added flexibility.

Why Not New Machinery?

Obviously, retrofitting older machinery is not always the answer. Sometimes, new machinery is in order for short-term and long-term productivity. Management needs to examine several issues closely, each one versus the cost of a new machine.

To begin, what is the flame cutting machine's general state of disrepair? Part of the reason why retrofitting older machinery costs less is that most retrofits primarily revolve around the control and drive system. However, when the older machine is in mass disrepair (structural frames, rails, torches, lifters, solenoids, cablings, etc.), fabricators may discover that a total retrofit may approach the cost of a new machine.

Added to that, when space is tight and fabricators are no longer using their optical tracing system, they might consider purchasing a new gantry machine without optical tracing to fit their space requirements better. For many manufacturers and fabricators, space is money.

Fabricators need to take a good, long look at why they need to retrofit their flame cutting machine. Is the reason based solely on machine downtime and immediate productivity shortcomings? Or does the reason include a dramatic change in fabrication emphasis? When fabricators want to upgrade a very old machine from oxyfuel to high-speed plasma and when they want to upgrade their production capabilities, a new machine with state-of-the-art capabilities may be in order. It may provide the flexibility and long-term capability they really need to grow.

Operator-Friendly CNC Retrofit

Finally, one of the best parts about new CNC technology is that it is easy to learn and operate.

In every case-history situation described in this article, operators who were sometimes reluctant were trained by the manufacturer within three or four days.

Within several months, each operator became proficient. In addition, some became more satisfied with their job responsibilities and could not imagine performing their duties without the new technology.

Chapter 4   Waterjet

Waterjet cutting systems: Using high pressure for clean cutting

Traveling at more than twice the speed of sound, a high-energy water stream has a profound effect on most materials, cutting them cleanly. This includes the production of high-visibility products such as automobile dashboard panels and corrugated containers and less noticeable products such as aircraft wing struts and bulletproof Kevlar® panels for armored vehicles.

Increasing numbers of materials are being cut or trimmed to shape by the power of water, resulting in one of the fastest growing cutting technologies — waterjet cutting.

Early Development

This concept of using a fluid, pressurized in some cases up to 60,000 pounds per square inch (PSI), was commercialized in 1971. Since then, waterjet cutting has expanded into almost every industrial sector, cutting disposable diapers, printed circuit boards, fiberglass, instrument panels, food products, and shoe leather.

In the early 1980s, the entrainment of an abrasive into the water stream enabled fluid jet cutting of metals. This technology, hydroabrasive jet cutting, is now being used to cut aluminum, stainless steel, titanium, INCONEL® alloys, and a variety of high-strength alloys and traditionally difficult-to-machine materials.

In fact, abrasive jet cutting has proved to be a universal answer to the cutting problems encountered in the aerospace industry's ongoing development of newer, tougher, more complex composite materials and alloys.

In the production of an ultrahigh-pressure water jet, clean water is first pressurized by a booster pump to approximately 150 PSI, then filtered and fed to the intensifier pump. The is an hydraulically-driven, pressure-compensated, reciprocating, double-acting type pump.

Pressurized hydraulic oil is alternately fed to opposite sides of a large piston, causing it to reciprocate and forcing smaller-diameter plungers to compress water in each of the high-pressure water cylinders on either side of the large oil piston.

INCONEL® is a trademark of the Inco family of companies.

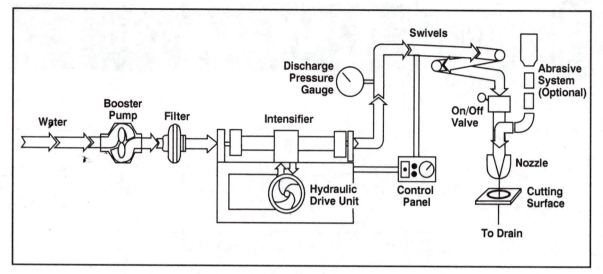

Figure 13-1. These are the basic elements of the waterjet cutting streamline system.

Movement of the large oil piston against the water in contact with the plunger causes a multiplication of water pressure by a factor approximately equal to the ratio of the annular surface area of the oil piston to the surface area of the water plunger. Depending upon the application, the selected intensification ratio can vary from 12:1 up to 40:1. This ratio dictates the distribution of available HP to water pressure and water flowrate.

For example, in a system with a 40:1 ratio, 1,250 PSI hydraulic oil will generate water pressure of 50,000 PSI.

High-pressure check valves restrict high-pressure water output until cylinder water pressure exceeds the pressure of the water already discharged. For a system operating at 55,000 PSI, the water will be compressed by 12 percent by volume before exiting the high-pressure cylinder.

Figure 13-1 shows the basic elements of a waterjet cutting streamline system.

The high-pressure water then passes through an attenuator, which acts both as a pressure surge absorber and as an accumulator, to provide a constant high-pressure water supply to the cutting nozzle. For safety purposes, a calibrated high-pressure rupture disk is used to guard against system over-pressurization.

Also, a pneumatically-operated dump valve is provided to safely bleed off high water pressure in the discharge system when emergency stop is activated.

The high-pressure water then passes through specially-treated, stainless steel, high-pressure tubing rated for 120,000 PSI burst pressure. If articulation of the cutting nozzle is required, a whip (flexible high-pressure tubing) and swivels (rotary unions) are used to allow the required degrees of freedom.

The cutting nozzle is controlled by a pneumatic valve, switching the high-pressure water on or off almost instantaneously in response to either manual or computer control, as with any conventional machine tool.

High-pressure water is thus supplied to the nozzle tube in which an orifice is mounted. This tiny orifice is constructed of synthetic sapphire material and has a small drill hole, through which the water is forced. The geometry of this hole, typically .004 inch to .014 inch, combined with pressure in the nozzle tube up to 55,000 PSI, results in a jet stream exiting the orifice at more than twice the speed of sound.

The waterjet stream cuts cleanly through organic materials without dulling or crushing. Using as

Waterjet Cutting Glossary

• **Articulation of the Cutting Nozzle:** Movement of the nozzle in one, two, or three dimensions. A robot arm, for example, could move the waterjet nozzle in five axes of motion.

• **Attenuator:** A device used to baffle or dampen a pulsating high-pressure water signal.

• **Entrained:** The abrasive particles are drawn into the waterjet stream and are mixed with high-speed water.

• **Kerf Width:** The kerf is the material removed from the production during cutting. The kerf width is the width of material removed and is generally small when using a waterjet.

• **Orifice:** A small object, generally made of synthetic sapphire material, which has a small (0.004 to 0.010 inch) diameter hole strategically drilled into it. The water is forced through this hole at speeds exceeding twice the speed of sound. This results in a narrow high-speed jet which has enough energy to cut through certain materials.

• **Reciprocate:** To move backward and forward in the same line, in a repetitive motion.

little as five gallons of water per hour, a waterjet can cut many materials faster and with less expense than conventional knives, often leaving a better surface finish and a higher-quality cut.

Because no transverse force is applied to the part being cut, the need for complex fixturing is reduced or eliminated. The low contact force of the waterjet minimizes crushing at the cut edge and can thereby reduce system downtime resulting from material jams caused by conventional knife-cutting operations.

Applications

An abrasive, typically garnet, can be entrained into the waterjet after it exits the sapphire orifice. The resulting slurry mixture is focused through an additional nozzle, resulting in an abrasive waterjet (AWJ) or hydroabrasive jet.

This jet can cut through up to 8 inches of high shear strength materials, such as steel, with no heat or material distortion. To change from waterjet cutting to hydroabrasive cutting requires only the exchange of nozzle bodies.

Abrasive jets are used for:

1. Cutting aircraft parts from materials such as Hastalloy® X, titanium, INCONEL® alloy, and metal matrix composites.

2. Cutting panels for the defense industry from materials such as Kevlar®, armor plate, and fiber-reinforced plastics (FRP).

3. Cutting stainless steel, high-carbon steel, nickel alloys, and metals with low machinability.

Jet Cutting Systems

Jet cutting systems can vary in size from 15 HP up to 500 HP, depending upon their specific application.

One intensifier can supply high-pressure water to a number of cutting nozzles. The size of the system will depend on the number of nozzles, orifice size, the desired operating pressure, and the required cutting conditions such as speed, kerf width, and edge quality.

The attainable cutting speed will depend on the material being cut, the thickness of the material being cut, and the edge quality required. In general, industrial waterjets use orifices between .004 inch and .010 inch in diameter, which require from 4 to 25 HP respectively.

Hydroabrasive jets operate with .010 inch to

The Hastalloy® trademark is owned by Haynes Corporation.

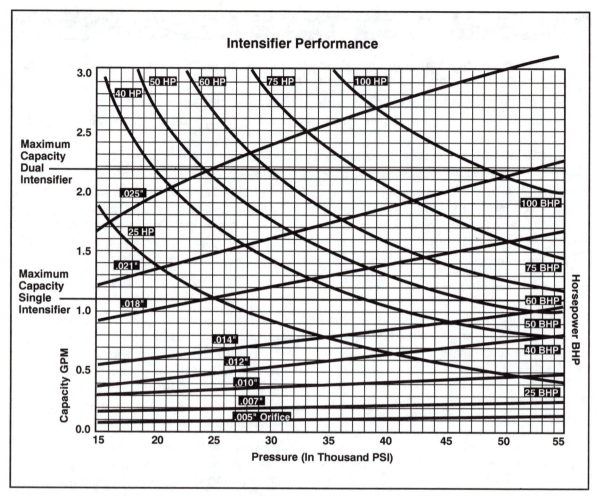

Figure 13-2. Here is a comparison of flowrate versus pressure versus horsepower, showing the water flowrate through particular diameter orifices at given pressures and horsepower required.

.014 inch diameter orifices, requiring 25 HP to 50 HP, at 50,000 PSI. **Figure 13-2** shows a comparison of flowrate versus pressure versus HP. The figure illustrates the water flowrate through particular diameter orifices at given pressures and the HP required to generate that flowrate.

For many applications, jet cutting can improve the process economy. For waterjet systems, the savings lie in the improved quality of the end product, flexibility of the cutting tool, and the elimination of environmental hazards such as dust.

In hydroabrasive cutting, time and materials savings can be realized through the narrow kerf width and the elimination of work hardening, heat-affected zones (HAZs), and, often, secondary finishing processes.

Computer numerically-controlled (CNC) water-jet and hydroabrasive cutting machines are becoming more commonplace in industry, using the omnidirectional nature of the jet to contour cut any type of flat stock. For trimming three-dimensional parts, five-axis gantry and pedestal-type robots are frequently used.

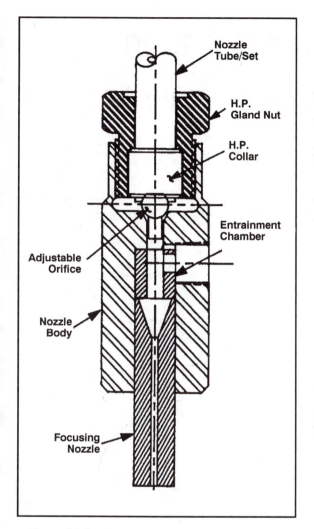

Figure 13-3. The nozzle assembly is illustrated here.

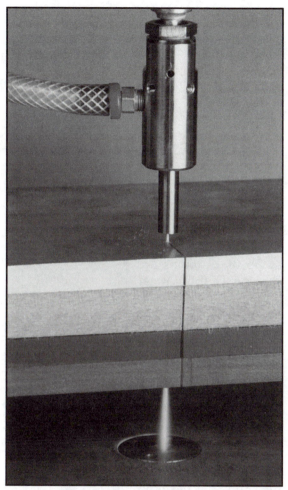

This shows hydroabrasive jet cutting of four layers of material at once. The top layer is .5 inch aluminum, followed by ¾ -inch Kevlar, .5-inch glass, and 5-inch Phenolic on the bottom.

Developments in Hydroabrasive Cutting

In hydroabrasive cutting before 1988, the operator had to align the focusing nozzle to the orifice each time a nozzle was changed. The tiny size of the orifice, along with uncontrollable inaccuracies in its manufacture and mounting, led to misalignment.

If the orifice was not perfectly centered and aligned, the resultant stream would lose significant energy in passing through contact with the tube walls. As a result, aligning the focusing tube to the waterjet stream was often time-consuming.

Today, a special nozzle body is available in which the diamond orifice is aligned to the nozzle initially and thereafter remains automatically aligned to any new nozzle (see **Figure 13-3**). This has led to accuracy, life, and speed improvements which result in better quality parts and a lower cost per cutting inch.

Procedure optimization and hardware improvements in abrasive waterjet cutting systems

A brasive waterjet (AWJ) cutting works by combining a focused jet of ultrahigh pressure [up to 55,000 pounds per square inch (PSI)] water with granular abrasives to form an extremely powerful means of cutting and piercing almost all hard materials, such as metals, composites, glass, and ceramics.

AWJ technology has matured considerably over the past two years to become a widely used, reliable machining process. Research and development continues to push the technology toward fully-automated systems. The goal is to achieve the highest efficiency with no operator guesswork.

AWJs offer advantages over other nontraditional machining methods. These advantages include:

1. No heat-affected zones (HAZs) on the cut materials.

2. Omnidirectional cutting capability to all types of materials.

3. Low cutting forces, usually less than 5 pounds vertically.

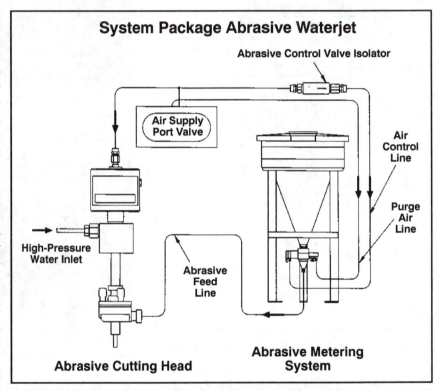

Figure 14-1. The basic system components of an AWJ cutting system include the abrasive metering system and the abrasive cutting head.

4. Generally fewer process steps.

5. Smaller kerf width than plasma or routing.

6. Tight tolerance cutting.

7. Very simple or sometimes no tooling required.

8. Reliable, repeatable part production.

This article includes an overview of the abrasive metering system, the cutting head, and accessories.

Basic System

The basic system components of an AWJ cutting system include the abrasive metering system and the abrasive cutting head (see **Figure 14-1**). Also needed for an AWJ system is a catcher to confine and dissipate the spent abrasive jet. The components are integrated into any number of motion devices to produce the cut parts required for a variety of applications.

The abrasive metering system consists of the abrasive hopper, the abrasive, the abrasive metering valve, and the abrasive delivery line. Since high-velocity abrasive particles are what actually removes material, the reliability and cutting efficiency of AWJ cutting depends on the smooth operation of the abrasive metering system.

The hopper stores the clean, dry abrasive for use when cutting. High-quality, well-screened garnet abrasives — typically 50 to 120 mesh size — are needed for consistent AWJ cutting. Wet or poor-quality abrasives have poor flow characteristics. Since abrasive grains remove material, surface finish depends on smooth flow.

Attached directly to the exit port of the hopper is the abrasive metering valve. Its function is to turn the flow of abrasive on and off, to meter the amount of abrasive used, and to purge the abrasive feed line of any transient water when the AWJ is not in use. Though vibration has been used to induce metering, gravity — being rather consistent — has proven to be the most dependable method.

Working in conjunction with the abrasive metering system is the abrasive cutting head (see **Figure 14-2**). The abrasive cutting head consists of the high-pressure valve actuator, valve body, nozzle body extension tube, waterjet orifice, abrasive mixing chamber, and mixing tube.

The high-pressure valve activator is pneumatically-operated with its operation tied into that of the abrasive metering valve. In other words, when the cutting head is activated to begin the flow of high-

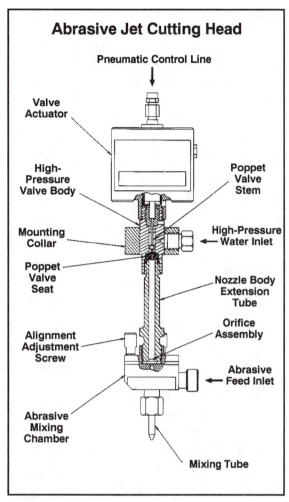

Figure 14-2. The abrasive cutting head works in conjunction with the abrasive metering system.

pressure water, the abrasive metering valve is simultaneously opened to begin the flow of abrasive. This valve is normally closed, so if compressed air is lost, the valve turns off, not on.

The high-pressure water flows through the sapphire or diamond orifice of .010 inch to .020 inch diameter into the mixing chamber and out through the mixing tube. As the water enters the mixing chamber, it creates an area of partial vacuum (or venturi), which draws the metered flow of abrasive particles through the abrasive feed line and into the mixing chamber. The abrasive is accelerated like a bullet out of a rifle by the waterjet and creates the high-energy abrasive jet cutting stream. This focused stream exits the cutting head through the mixing tube.

The mixing chamber assembly includes alignment screws and a gimballed mount. These alignment screws enable the user to align the waterjet stream quickly to the center of the mixing tube. The alignment is required to achieve the most powerful cutting stream and to maintain long mixing tube life.

Improvements in the rate of wear of the consumable materials of the abrasive jet cutting head have enhanced its use for continuous cutting and tight tolerance applications. Previous cutting head technology required the replacement of wear parts, particularly the mixing tube, and realignment of the cutting head generally every two to eight hours, depending on the application and the cutting accuracy required. This frequent changing of worn mixing tubes required constant operator attention and much system downtime.

The extended mixing tube life of 100 hours permits a single mixing tube to be used to cut parts at the end of a shift within several thousandths of an inch tolerance to those cut at the start of the shift, without any adjustments to the machine tool for kerf compensation. This translates to less downtime per shift, higher throughput potential, and tighter cut part tolerances.

Catchers

Abrasive jet cutting develops a large amount of energy [up to 50 horsepower (HP)] at the cutting nozzle. As much as 75 percent of that energy may be retained in the stream after it has passed through a cut. Something is needed to stop, or catch, this jet.

Three basic types of catchers are available to dissipate this energy:

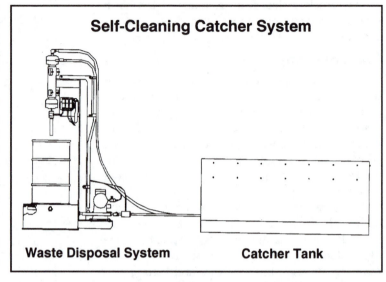

Self-Cleaning Catcher System

Waste Disposal System   **Catcher Tank**

Figure 14-3. The self-cleaning catcher is used for work envelopes anywhere from 18 inches square to 6 feet by 10 feet.

1. Room catchers
2. Tank catchers
3. Compact catchers

Each catcher dissipates the remaining energy of the abrasive jet stream and collects the spent abrasives and kerf material.

Room Catcher. A room catcher is the simplest type of catcher. Users machining complex 3-D parts sometimes will enclose the entire gantry robot and workpiece. A drain is put in the center of the room. Parts are fixed about 3 feet off the floor and cut. This approach can be loud and messy and is not very common with today's systems.

Tank Catcher. A tank catcher is a large steel container permanently positioned beneath the work surface within the work area of the AWJ motion equipment. Tank catchers are supplied for applications in which the workpiece is stationary and the end effector is mobile and capable of horizontal or near-horizontal cuts, such as with a 2- or 3-axis gantry machine. This is the most common of the basic catcher types.

Tank catchers are filled with at least 30 inches of water to absorb residual energy. They can also be filled with other energy-absorbing media in addition to the water — typically steel balls. The combination of "self-healing," energy-absorbing media and water is preferred over only water in installations which require quieter operation. Tank catchers also have material supports similar to those used with other beam-type cutters such as lasers or plasma. The most common approach is to use commercially-available, replaceable steel grating or steel slats atop the catcher to support the material. Supports can be as simple as resting the material directly on the steel balls or as elaborate as dedicated palletized fixturing.

When using a standard tank catcher, the spent abrasives and kerf material settle out and remain in the tank, while the water drains off. The tank must then be cleaned manually, perhaps every two to six months, as it fills with solids. This clean-out requires that the system be shut down until cleaning is complete. Frequency of cleaning varies based on system usage.

The largest breakthrough in tank catcher technology has been in the emergence of the self-cleaning catcher with which manual shoveling is eliminated and no associated downtime is incurred (see **Figure 14-3**). This catcher is used for work envelopes anywhere from 18 inches square to 6 feet by 10 feet.

The system consists of a catcher tank with a properly sloping bottom. This sloped tank is filled with water (and, at the discretion of the user, a layer of steel balls). The spent abrasive and kerf materials drain out of the catcher. These waste materials then go through a particulate separation device where the abrasive particles are separated out, and the clean water is pumped back into the catcher to provide a constant supply of flush water. The solids are dropped into a 55-gallon holding drum. Any excess clean overflow water is directed to drain. When the holding drum becomes full, it is removed and replaced with an empty drum. Drums are changed easily with no system downtime.

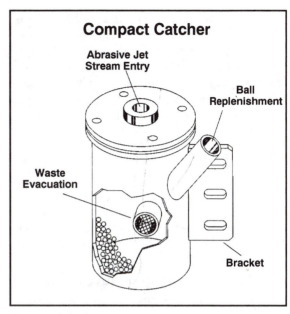

Figure 14-4. Compact catchers are small containers filled with "self-healing," energy-absorbing media, typically stainless steel balls.

This catcher technology is useful for many common types of cutting applications. It makes the disposal of spent abrasive less time-consuming and less labor-intensive. It also facilitates the disposal of hazardous waste material if hazardous materials are being cut.

Compact Catchers. These catchers (see **Figure 14-4**) are small containers filled with energy-absorbing media, typically stainless steel balls. These catchers are usually mounted to move with the cutting head via a C-frame bracket and are used primarily in three-dimensional machining.

After the abrasive jet stream passes through the workpiece, it enters the catcher and strikes the steel balls, sending them into motion. The continuous collision and agitation of the balls effectively absorbs and dissipates residual AWJ energy. The catcher bodies are not wear items, but the stainless steel balls are. The steel balls are consumed at a predictable rate (usually 1 pound per hour) and are automatically replenished from a small reservoir on the catcher.

The process waste produced by AWJ cutting is

a slurry consisting of water and solid sediments, which are minute particles of abrasive grit, kerf material, and catcher ball fragments. To prevent the slurry from separating and clogging the outlet drain of compact catchers, a vacuum and waste separation system is supplied to evacuate process waste constantly and transfer it to a waste separation and disposal system, like the one shown in Figure 14-3.

Compact catcher bodies are designed as small as possible to function in tight spaces. Compact catchers are suited for robotic applications in which a low-profile cutting head is required. Following special operating procedures also allows compact catchers to be used in nonhorizontal cutting applications.

Options for Full System Automation

When integrating an AWJ onto a robotic system, care must be taken to ensure proper operation of both the abrasive metering system and the abrasive cutting head. A number of system options exist that are well suited for multiaxis cutting installations to make them as automated and trouble-free as possible.

Automated Metering Valve. Currently available is an automated metering valve. Its function is the same as that of the standard manual valve — to turn off and on the abrasive flow and to meter the amount of abrasive used for cutting applications. This automated valve can be programmed into the cutting program directly on the controller of the robotic system. The operator never needs to touch the valve for adjustment, but instead adjusts the flow as on another machine axis.

Performance Monitor. Also available is the performance monitor, which detects abrasive flow, orifice health, and water pressure. This monitor is attached to the cutting head and indicates when cutting head performance exceeds a user-defined range. Exceeding the preset limits can trigger a system shut-down or sound a warning before any workpiece damage occurs. This is invaluable when cutting laminated composites such as graphite or Kevlar®, or brittle parts such as glass, stone, or ceramics.

Bulk Abrasive Transfer System. Another system enhancement available is a bulk abrasive transfer system. This system transports abrasive from a large, remotely-placed storage hopper to a smaller metering hopper situated relatively close to the abrasive jet cutting head. A bulk transfer system is useful when the size of the cutting system is large.

The bulk transfer system contains sensors to indicate low abrasive levels in the storage hopper. The abrasive is transported continuously from the storage hopper to the small metering hopper with the use of compressed air. Abrasive is pushed through the system piping to the metering hopper with the use of low-pressure compressed air. The low pressure minimizes component wear from the abrasive particles. A hopper close to the cutting head has the advantage of providing consistent abrasive flows for all required cutting parameters.

Abrasive Jet Cartridge. This prealigned cartridge consists of a sapphire orifice, the abrasive mixing chamber, and the mixing tube. It is useful for multiaxis cutting systems. This tool has been developed to cut the amount of operator involvement with the cutting system to a minimum and improve part production accuracy.

Cutting can begin as soon as the cartridge is attached to the extension tube of the abrasive jet cutting head. No alignment of jet stream to mixing tube is needed. The tool centerpoint (TCP) remains consistent from one abrasive jet cartridge to another, making it very useful for three-dimensional cutting.

Part Quality Improvements

For those applications in which the surface frosting created during AWJ machining is unacceptable, a dehazing device is now available.

The device attaches to the cutting head and minimizes the surface frosting by stripping away the low-powered shroud that surrounds the high-velocity abrasive jet stream. The dehazing device also minimizes noise and airborne abrasive grit. It is helpful when cutting brass or other materials with shiny surfaces.

Database Development

A large emphasis has been placed on improving the components of the AWJ system. Equally important is the need to understand the proper way to operate an AWJ effectively for each application.

Many variables affect the performance of an AWJ cutting system. Among the most important are water pressure, abrasive flowrate, abrasive type, waterjet orifice size, mixing tube geometry, the type of material being cut, and the material thickness. Because these variables may be adjusted over a range of values, it is possible to operate an AWJ in a very inefficient manner.

To assist AWJ users in running their systems effectively, a computer software tool has been developed. The software offers AWJ users a simple yet powerful means of determining how to adjust an AWJ cutting system for superior performance. It accomplishes this with four main features:

1. It supplies recommended AWJ cutting data for commonly-cut materials. The software includes a list of process parameter settings, resulting cut speed, and surface quality for a variety of common materials. If a user is going to cut 2.54-centimeter (1-inch) thick stainless steel, the software data can indicate exactly how to cut it.

The data is given for:

* Material thickness ranging from 0.154 centimeter to 5.08 centimeters (0.060 inch to 2 inches).
* Water pressure in both 275,862 KPa (40 KPSI) and 344,828 KPa (50 KPSI)
* Cut speed of quality cut and separation cut
* Three standard orifice/mixing tube combinations

2. The software allows users to add their own materials and settings. The user data is then merged with the supplied data, ready to be referenced again at any time in the future.

3. A dual bar-graph compares costs per inch of cut to cut speed. Here, the user can see how much it costs per inch to cut the material with an AWJ system. The costs are accurate because users input their own labor, power, water, pump, and abrasive costs.

4. The software also includes a method for storing client and part information. This allows the users to list all their customers, the jobs performed, and the parameters previously used to cut the materials for those jobs. Everything needed to run a repeat job is at their fingertips.

Because the number of process variables and their possible ranges are so great in an AWJ system, it is important to find a way to optimize the cutting process. Through experience from theoretical insight and empirical testing, the range of the variables has been reduced to allow a user to begin cutting in a practical and efficient manner. These settings were arrived at after months of testing and empirical analysis of the AWJ cutting process.

For example, the size relationship between the orifice and mixing tube is very important. A mixing tube that is too large coupled with an orifice that is too small will not allow the abrasive to be accelerated properly. The inverse condition of a mixing tube that is too small coupled with an orifice that is too large will create frictional drag losses and poor abrasive entrainment. The orifice/mixing tube combinations listed in the software have been chosen to balance these two effects.

Most importantly, the abrasive flowrate, water pressure, orifice size, and material thickness have been matched to give the highest cutting speed at the lowest cost.

The experience and knowledge incorporated into the software can reduce the time needed to get an AWJ system operating efficiently. Combined with recent hardware improvements, the software can help in the continuing advancement of AWJ technology.

Conclusion

AWJ cutting continues to grow and is coming into its own as an alternative machining method. Recent improvements have brought the technology closer to the reality of full automation. Future research and product development will continue to address the issues of user friendliness and full automation. This process will continue to grow and mature in the coming years.

Fundamentals of waterjet technology: A discussion of high-pressure waterjet equipment selection for cutting and surface cleaning applications

The metal fabrication industry uses many cutting processes for varied applications. The most commonly used processes involve mechanical equipment such as cutting saws, cutting wheels, cutting wire, knives, snippers, and routers. These methods are generally used for medium- to light-gauge sheet metal and flat stocks. Material of medium to high thickness ranges such as plate and structural steel is burned by cutting processes such as oxyfuel, plasma arc, laser, etc.

The newest cutting process in metal fabrication is waterjet cutting. An ultrahigh-pressure, pencil-thin jet of water moving at up to three times the velocity of sound provides a very effective means of cutting metal sheets and plates.

The waterjet, with properly-designed cutting parameters, can cut through most materials of varied thicknesses with superior edge quality at a generally low cutting cost.

Water Power

Water compressed at ultrahigh pressures retains a very high level of kinetic energy. When this high pressure water at 55,000 to 60,000 pounds per square inch (PSI) is released through a small opening, it travels at very high speed of up to 1,900 miles per hour and releases its kinetic energy.

This energy has the erosion power to cut through a 3- to 4-inch-thick steel plate. The cutting or cleaning action of high-pressure water is generally referred to as the **compressive erosion process**.

The pressure and volume [gallons per minute (GPM)] of water determine the overall effect of the process. However, as the flowrate increases, the operating pressure drops. This, along with other application needs, has resulted in two types of high-pressure equipment.

Metal Cutting. Water can be pressurized by a pump called an intensifier. Here, the hydraulic pressure of oil is converted into the hydraulic pressure of water in a two-stage pumping process.

The size and ratio of the piston diameters of the oil and water pumps determine the level of water pressure achieved. The intensifier-type pumps are capable of achieving ultrahigh pressures up to 55,000 PSI with an estimated water flowrate of up to 2.8 GPM, using an orifice opening of up to 0.013 inch. The pumps with these general specifications and abrasive assist are usually used for metal cutting applications.

Surface Cleaning. A second type of pump uses the direct speed of the pump drive piston to generate water pressure. Pressure levels are regulated by the speed of piston and engine operation. These pumps can generate pressures up to 30,000 PSI.

This pressure is not high enough for metal cutting applications. However, the direct drive pumps generate high water flowrates of up to 130 GPM and can use large orifices with up to 0.040 inch at their opening. These pumps are generally used for metal descaling, deburring, and cleaning applications in the place of sand blasting, grit blasting, surface cleaning, etc.

Commercially-available ultra high-pressure pumps for metal cutting applications range from 25 horsepower (HP) to 150 HP. These pumps are capable of water flowrates ranging from 0.5 GPM to 3.8 GPM at maximum rated operating pressures.

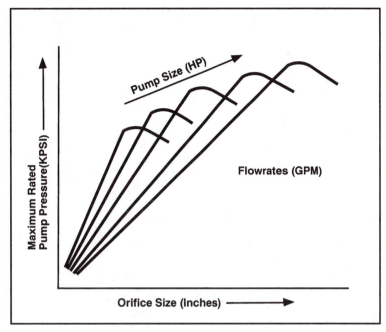

Figure 15-1. This graph shows water flowrate as a function of various pump sizes.

The low-pressure direct plunger driven pumps for cleaning and descaling applications are commercially available in a range from 75 HP to 215 HP. They can generate very high water flowrates ranging from 5 GPM to 130 GPM at pressure ranging from 2,000 PSI to 30,000 PSI.

Along with the intensifier/pump, other support equipment necessary to complete a cutting system includes:

1. Water treatment and filtration.
2. Booster pump.
3. Cutting head.
4. Abrasive dispensing system.
5. Cutting head manipulation.
6. Cutting table.
7. Water catcher.
8. Waste water processor.

Cutting Applications

Application engineering is a significant exercise in the selection of appropriately specified waterjet cutting equipment. A significant part of the up-front engineering is based on experience.

Equipment is available in many models and capacity ranges. The equipment must be appropriately sized to match the application needs. Failing to do so either makes a system too expensive with higher-than-necessary operating costs or lacking performance in the specific application for which it is intended.

The critical factor in specifying waterjet equipment is the determination of GPM at a pressure (KPSI) level and orifice size (inches) necessary to meet pre-established criteria for cutting performance. This is specified by the HP rating of the motor in the pump.

A pump of certain HP has a maximum GPM capacity at a given orifice size and at the rated maximum operating pressure. Increase of orifice size to achieve higher flowrate will cause pressure drop and therefore affect cutting performance, indicating the need for a higher HP pump. This correlation between flowrate, orifice size, and

Cutting Speed in Inches per Minute for Different Material Thicknesses					
	Thickness (in inches)				
Material	.031	.5	1.0	2.0	4.0
Aluminum Alloys	40	6	2.0	0.8	0.2
Brass	50	4	0.5	0.3	0.1
Carbon Steel	40	6	2.0	0.8	0.2
Copper	50	6	1.5	0.6	0.1
Heat-Resistant Alloys	40	5	1.5	0.8	0.1
Tool Steel	25	10	5.0	2.0	0.5
Stainless Steel	22	4	1.0	0.5	0.1
Titanium	32	6	2.0	0.8	0.02
INCONEL®	50	4	1.0	0.2	—

rated maximum pump pressure is shown in **Figure 15-1**.

Metals in general, and steel in particular, require an abrasive to be mixed in the waterjet for cutting. Three major areas must be considered while making an equipment selection for a specific cutting application:

1. **Material properties**
   * Hardness
   * Density
   * Thickness
   * Composition
   * Part geometry or shape

2. **Desired cutting performance**
   * Cycle time throughput
   * Edge finish
   * Kerf width
   * Kerf angle
   * Dimensional tolerances
   * Operating cost

Based on these requirements, operating process parameters are designed for the best performance. These parameters must be specified through tests and trial runs that simulate operating conditions.

3. **Operating parameters**
   * Operating water pressure
   * Orifice inside diameter (ID)
   * Nozzle ID
   * Nozzle length
   * Nozzle standoff
   * Type of abrasive
   * Abrasive particle size
   * Abrasive feed rate
   * Cutting speed rate

Technology Advantage

Although pressurized water technology has been around for quite some time, its popularity as a cutting process in the fabricating industry is relatively recent. New innovations in the design of high-pressure intensifier pumps has helped to increase applications of the technology in recent years.

High-pressure waterjet cutting technology has some significant advantages over conventional cutting methods. Some of these which have not been mentioned previously include:

1. It cuts all materials — metallic and nonmetallic — without the effect of heat on the cut edges.

2. It does not involve the environmental and safety problems of dust, chips, fumes, slag, heat, and fire.

3. It eliminates burrs, dross, oxidation, heat effect, kerf loss, and other quality problems.

4. It does not alter the metallurgical or mechanical properties of the metal cut edge because there is no heat effect. Therefore, stress relieving (annealing) is not necessary.

Every metal cutting application is unique. A thorough evaluation of the cutting criteria is therefore necessary for proper equipment selection.

INCONEL® is a trademark of the Inco family of companies.

The evaluation phase must include feasibility trials in which cutting is performed on the actual material and the cut part is tested for acceptability. The test material should be cut with cutting parameters appropriately simulated to meet in-plant production requirements. Materials tested under controlled laboratory conditions often fail quality requirements when subjected to the required production speeds and the environment of plant operations.

Such realistic simulated test facilities are available through job shops offering waterjet contract manufacturing services. Although such services are not free, it is a small price to pay to improve the reliability of the economic justification of such a project before making the necessary investment.

Improper selection of a waterjet cutting system has often resulted in a failed project. When properly selected, waterjet cutting technology is cost-effective, safe, and delivers a high-quality product in many metal cutting and surface cleaning applications.

Waterjet and laser methods offer alternatives for different applications: Factors to consider when choosing a cutting method

In the search for a low-cost way to cut high-quality parts from complex materials, manufacturers and job shop owners are comparing the costs and benefits of several state-of-the-art cutting methods. This article discusses two of them — lasers and abrasive waterjets (AWJs).

It took nearly 20 years for lasers to move from the laboratory to the shop floor. The first industrial laser was developed in 1966, but it was not until 1985 that small, low-maintenance, fast axial flow CO_2 lasers became an economical cutting alternative in many applications.

Economical waterjet cutting was made possible in 1973 with the development of a commercial intensifier pump that could pressurize water to 55,000 pounds per square inch (PSI).

The water is forced through a small sapphire orifice (typically 0.004 inch) to produce a high-velocity waterjet traveling at approximately three times the speed of sound. Pure waterjets were rapidly accepted for cutting many materials.

Within 10 years, a device was developed that entrains abrasives (usually garnet) into the water stream. This technique produces an AWJ that cuts whatever a laser can cut, and more.

Recent improvements in abrasive delivery and the development of long-wearing components have made this AWJ technology effective for cutting net or near-net shapes.

Laser or AWJ, or Both

Laser and AWJ processes have been shown to complement each other. In fact, it is becoming more common to see both systems in a single shop. These processes are gaining acceptance for cutting standard as well as exotic materials. The general similarities and differences between the two methods follow.

Similarities

Laser and AWJ share a number of characteristics. The similarities can be classified into the following areas:

1. Omnidirectional cutting
2. Low cutting force
3. Integration into motion equipment

Omnidirectional Cutting. Both AWJs and lasers can cut in any direction. The omnidirectional cutting attribute is common to all "beam type" cutters and enables the process to be integrated easily into numerically-controlled (NC) machines. This gives the flexibility of cutting many different shapes by simply changing the programmed tool path.

Low Cutting Force. AWJs and lasers both have very low cutting forces. The AWJ often exerts less than one pound of force onto the workpiece; the laser almost none. The workpiece and fixturing do not have to withstand high cutting tool forces, resulting in simplified and more flexible fixturing.

Integration into Motion Equipment. The same ordinary motion equipment used for the flame and plasma processes can easily be used with AWJs and lasers with little or no modification. However, many of the AWJ and laser manufacturers have developed their own motion equipment that meets the needs of each particular process, concentrating on greater motion accuracy, ease of operation, durability, and low maintenance.

The configuration of many laser and AWJ machines will move the cutting tool in the X and Y directions with the material stationary. Other configurations include the material moving in one axis and the cutting head in the other, and the material moving in both the X and Y directions (axis) while the head is stationary. The stationary-head technique, though used with the laser process, is seldom used for the AWJ process.

Not all applications for the AWJ and laser processes are for two-dimensional parts. For the three-dimensional work, five to six axes of programmable articulation are employed. These multiaxis machines have delicate wrists with low payload capacities.

Both the AWJ and laser have relatively light cutting heads, enabling easy integration onto these sophisticated systems. The laser cutting head typically weighs between 40 and 100 pounds, with no reactive force (backthrust) during operation. The AWJ cutting head weighs between 10 and 15 pounds. The maximum backthrust using the largest typical abrasive jet orifice is under 20 pounds. The lighter the cutting head, the faster the manipulator can move while maintaining accuracy.

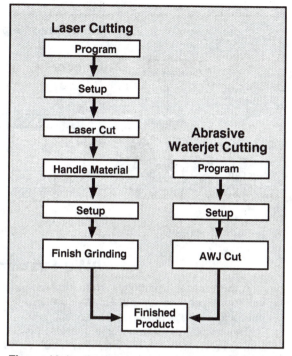

Figure 16-1. This flow chart comparison applies whenever a laser cut part must be machined to remove heat-affected or oxidized zones.

Differences

In many cases, the capital and operating costs of both laser and AWJ technology systems are similar for a given application, but their capabilities are quite different. The differences can be classified into the following areas:

1. Material thickness
2. Edge quality
3. Material versatility
4. Process versatility

The primary advantages of lasers over AWJs are greater cutting speeds and tighter tolerances in cutting thin metals (less than 0.250 inch).

The primary advantages of AWJs over lasers are the ability to cut greater material thickness, the ability to cut heat-sensitive materials, and the absence of a heat-affected zone (HAZ) on the cut surface (see **Figure 16-1**).

Intensifier Pump Working Principle

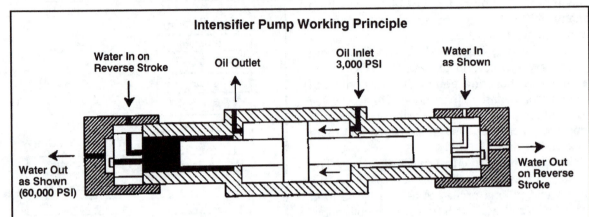

Figure 16-2.

AWJ System Component

A basic waterjet cutting system consists of a water-pressure booster and filtration system, the intensifier pump, a nozzle, and a catcher.

The booster increases incoming water pressure to the level required by the intensifier — 65 to 80 PSI. The filtration system extends the operating life of pump seals, system check valves, and orifices by filtering out damaging particulate matter from ordinary incoming tap water. The intensifier is an hydraulically-driven reciprocating pump (see **Figure 16-2**).

To this basic ultrahigh-pressure water generating system, AWJ cutting systems require the addition of an abrasive delivery system and a specially-designed abrasive cutting head.

It must be noted that part tolerances are a product of many factors, such as motion equipment accuracy, cutting process accuracy, fixturing, and flatness of base material.

Material Thickness. The typical laser has difficulty cutting materials over 0.25 inch thick. It is unusual to see successful, productive cutting of materials 0.5 inch thick or greater.

Also, as the cutting speed decreases for those materials approaching 0.25 inch thick, the size of the HAZ increases. If the HAZ is unacceptable, costly secondary operations are incurred to remove this layer.

AWJs cut almost any material up to 8 inches thick, and they cut multiple parts from stacks of thin materials, such as shim stock.

Edge Quality. For sheet metal cutting in thicknesses less than 0.125 inch, lasers can produce parts to tight tolerances with some HAZs. Thicker materials tend to yield a greater degree of affected area. Sometimes, this area is acceptable for the final part application. Other times, a grinding operation may be required to remove this layer.

The AWJ produces a cut to tight tolerances that is free of HAZs or mechanical stresses. Warpage induced by machining is nonexistent. Since a fine sand-like abrasive is used to remove material, the cut surface obtained with the AWJ process is sandblasted in appearance.

A case study in 1990 found that the cost of edge-grinding 0.030-inch silicon wafers made up 70 percent of the cost of the finished wafer. The wafer cut with the AWJ needed no additional finishing and cost $0.184 per part. The laser and subsequent edge-grinding cost $0.596 per part. This, of course, is a very specific application but does illustrate the point.

Material Versatility. The laser removes material thermally, while the AWJ removes material by high-speed erosion with a fine abrasive particle. These two methods are effective for cutting most thin metals. However, heat-sensitive materials cause a problem for lasers.

Some of today's composite materials that use epoxy to bond laminate layers or thick cloth-like materials cannot be effectively cut by the laser. The AWJ does not use heat to remove the material and has proven effective in cutting composites used in the aerospace industry and other commercial applications.

Process Versatility. Both the laser and the AWJ are versatile devices. By changing operating parameters or modifying system hardware, each process can perform other operations besides just cutting.

The laser can cut, pierce, weld, and perform noncontact marking and selective heat treatment. The AWJ is being used for cutting, piercing, etching, cleaning, turning, and hydromilling.

Some of these process capabilities for both the laser and the AWJ require modifications to the systems, while others do not. For example, a laser can etch a material it has just cut by altering parameters (traverse speed, power, and optics). This is also true of the AWJ (when the traverse speed, pressure, and abrasive flowrate parameters are altered). Also, the AWJ can be transformed into a pure waterjet system in seconds for use in cutting thin nonmetallics, removing paint, and cleaning.

There are two other considerations worth mentioning when comparing lasers and AWJs. They are cutting speed and catcher's requirements.

Cutting Speed

The cutting speed of a laser for a given thin metal is often higher than the AWJ. However, the real limitation in cutting speed is usually induced by the motion equipment, not the cutting process. If the motion equipment can contour a complex shape to required tolerance at 50 inches per minute (IPM) at best, then either process will do.

Almost any gantry-styled motion equipment can travel fairly quickly in linear moves — up to 600 IPM is not uncommon. However, this same machine may have to slow to one-tenth the linear speed to contour a small, intricate shape. As controlled motion technology improves, lasers will become more and more desirable for machining small, complex shapes in thin metals.

Catchers*

A catcher is a device which supports the material during and after cutting and holds the waste material for disposal.

The laser does not require an elaborate catcher system, since the beam only has intense heating ability at its focal region. Typically, a small catcher or tray is needed to collect the molten globules of material for disposal.

The real problem is the fumes given off when melting (cutting) the material. Though these fumes are not necessarily toxic, they can pose health dangers or discomfort to the operator and those in the vicinity of the machine. It is common practice to ventilate these fumes out of the work areas.

AWJs do require some form of a catcher device as the high-velocity abrasive jet beam can remain powerful after cutting through the material. A catcher must be in place to dissipate the kinetic energy of the stream and collect the slurry, which consists of water, abrasive, and the kerf material of the cut part.

A properly-designed catcher will also decrease the noise level during operation to well within state and federal requirements.

No fumes are generated in this almost heat-free cutting, and all the kerf material is swept away with the water/abrasive slurry. Therefore, no ventilation is required.

Generally, lasers and AWJs use similar techniques for material support. The supports themselves are often sacrificial in that they can be worn during cutting and require occasional replacement. Examples of support media include pins, slats, grating, and rollers. Special applications may use other techniques.

* *For more information on types of catchers, see "Procedure optimization and hardware improvements in abrasive waterjet cutting," page 106.*

Chapter 5 — Other Technologies

Profile cutting with CNC software: Gaining productivity through computer technology

Modern computer numerically-controlled (CNC) profile cutting equipment delivers features that make the production of arbitrary shapes from sheet or plate material precise, repeatable, and efficient.

Profile cutting machines are classified as two-axis machine tools, with the cutting head capable of movement in the X and Y axes independently. Most profile cutting machines use plasma or oxy-fuel as the cutting process, and many have both processes available.

Other processes like laser, waterjet, and router are also being used with increasing frequency.

The CNC is the specialized computer that is used to control the activity of the profile cutting machine. It governs the activation and deactivation of the cutting and marking processes as well as the actual movement of the cutting head in both the X and Y axes. The controller reads a list of relatively simplistic instructions called a CNC program and causes the cutting machine to sequentially perform each command instruction.

Today's CNCs have features designed to make profile cutting machines more versatile and easier to use. Some of these features are:

1. Automatic kerf compensation.
2. Plate alignment.
3. Libraries of standard shapes.
4. Auto ignition and auto height control.
5. Graphic displays with torch tracking.
6. Simple interactive nesting.

The use of standard shape libraries or controller-based nesting is one way to meet spontaneous production needs.

As good as many of these controller features are, the real key to maximizing the potential benefits of CNC profile cutting is the integrated use of CNC part development and nesting software. With all of the capabilities of modern CNCs, it is easy to lose sight of the primary function of the cutting machine: production.

In most cases, productivity is better served by removing the CNC part development and nesting processes from the production machine.

CNC Software

CNC software are computer programs specifically designed to develop the instructions understood by the CNC profile cutting machine controller to generate the desired part geometry. This software can be divided into three major categories:

1. Part development
2. Nesting
3. Utility

Part development programs are used to translate the geometric requirements of individual piece parts into the CNC instructions that will produce that geometry. This involves defining the interior and exterior cutting profiles, as well as any ancillary functions, such as marking.

Nesting involves arranging various quantities of individual part geometries on sheets of material by changing the position and/or orientation of the originally-programmed part.

Utility programs can cover a wide range of functions, from part verification to specialized computer-to-CNC communication [direct numerical control (DNC)], from specialized process control, such as contour beveling, to part and plate inventory systems.

Until the early 1980s, CNC software was only available on expensive mainframe or minicomputer equipment. Because of the complexity and site-specific nature of these large computer systems, CNC software also tended to be expensive. The combination of expensive computer hardware and software usually meant that only large companies could afford to use CNC software to program their CNC profile cutting machines.

Like so many other areas of business, the development of the personal computer (PC) over the last 10 years has revolutionized CNC manufacturing software.

The standardized operating system (MS/PC DOS) of PCs has allowed developers to create CNC software that requires little or no customization to run on a client's hardware. Inexpensive hardware and standardized software has allowed even small firms to benefit from CNC software.

Part Development Software

One of the primary steps in the use of CNC profile cutting equipment is to develop the necessary CNC instructions to generate a given part. The part development system is responsible for generating these instructions so that the part has the desired geometry.

The earliest part creation systems were really no more than a keyboard terminal attached to a paper tape punch. This allowed the operator to punch each instruction onto the program tape.

This method of part creation required the operator to completely understand the CNC language as well as how to calculate the required coordinates of the endpoints of line and arc motions at intersections and tangencies.

CNC editors were the next major step in PC-based CNC software. A CNC editor stored the CNC instructions for a part program in the memory of the computer. The ability to edit or change CNC instructions simplified the tedious task of creating a complete part program.

After the CNC program was developed, it could be punched out on paper tape, transferred to the cutting machine by DNC, or even copied to a floppy disk that could be directly read by the controller.

As CNC editors evolved, features like on-screen verification of part geometry and geometric math functions were added. This allowed the development of CNC programs for complex profiles to be generated more quickly and accurately.

Parametric programming can be defined as a method of developing part geometry whereby the program prompts the operator for the necessary dimensions, performs any necessary calculations based on that data, and then automatically creates the CNC part program.

Parametric programming can be used in the development of two-dimensional parts, as well as in the flat plate development of three-dimensional parts. Parametric programming can be used for everything from rectangle to round transitions for piping systems to the development of the hull plates of ocean-going ships.

PC-based computer-aided design (CAD) systems are an effective way to create and draw part geometry. Unfortunately, it has been necessary to reenter that geometry into a CNC editor to make the CNC part program.

Recently, CAD interface software has been developed to extract part geometry directly from the CAD drawing and create the CNC part program. These CAD interfaces can work as supplements to the CAD system or as stand-alone programs.

Some programs simply automate the process of developing the cutting path, while more sophisticated systems can develop complete CNC part programs without any operator intervention.

Nesting Software

Nesting, as it applies to CNC programming, is the process of arranging individual part geometries on sheet or plate material to optimize the use of that material. A single CNC program is then produced to cut all nested parts. Parts are usually rotated and positioned during the nesting process.

The two major categories of CNC nesting software are:

1. Interactive systems.

2. Automatic systems.

Interactive systems assist the process of nesting by allowing the operator to manipulate individual parts by moving and rotating them on an image of the plate. The operator must decide on the optimal placement of each part to be nested.

Modern interactive nesting systems have advanced features such as mouse control and automatic checking for insufficient part separation.

Automatic systems mathematically evaluate part geometry and then, based on the nesting methodology used, place the parts on the plate in an optimized manner. Usually, the only operator

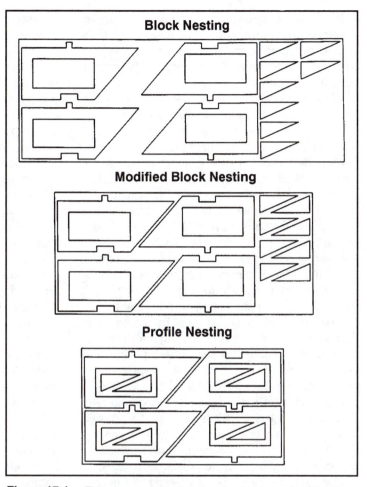

Figure 17-1. This shows a typical nest generated by each of the three major types of automatic nesting methodology.

input required is to set the nesting parameters, such as plate size and part separation.

Because of their automated nature, fully automatic nesting systems are well-suited to integration with Just-In-Time (JIT) manufacturing.

The three major types of automatic nesting methodology are:

1. Block (or rectangular).

2. Modified block.

3. Profile.

Figure 17-1 shows a typical nest generated by each type.

Block nesting involves drawing a rectangular envelope around the part to be nested and then placing that part on the plate so that its envelope does not interfere with the envelope of any other parts already nested.

While block nesting is fast — because of the limited number of mathematical calculations performed — it almost always results in the lowest material utilization of the three methods.

Modified block nesting improves upon the block method through the use of optimization techniques. One common method is to group pairs of parts together so that the envelope of the pair is less than the sum of the individual part envelopes. After the pairing has been determined, the nesting process is the same as block nesting.

Modified block nesting methods usually produce better material utilization than block nesting with only a slight reduction in nesting speed.

Profile nesting is the most mathematically demanding of the three nesting methods. It involves examining the actual part profile and how it can best be positioned with respect to the profiles of all of the already nested part profiles.

Most true profile nesting systems can also take advantage of interior voids in parts as the possible location for smaller parts. The increased nesting time required by true profile nesting methods is almost always offset by material utilization gains.

The following case studies illustrate the impact that the use of CNC profile cutting equipment and software has had on two very different businesses.

Case Study 1

Case Study 1 is of Gibraltar Steel Products in Buffalo, New York. The company is a plate and structural steel service center which provides profile cutting services.

The service center installed its first CNC profile cutting machine in 1990. It still has four numerically-controlled (NC) optical tracing machines in production use.

Company management saw CNC equipment and software as the way to reduce costs associated with the drafting and use of paper templates. Part development and nesting have allowed the company to expand the custom profile cutting portion of its business.

CNC part development at the service center is done with a CNC editor. By using just one CNC profile cutting machine, drafting time for the production of templates has been reduced by 60 percent.

Templates are discarded after use because of storage problems. CNC part designs for customer jobs are saved on disk for future use.

The service center uses an interactive nesting system to nest parts for its CNC cutting machine. The ability to nest complex shapes easily and to use the cutout areas (drops) inside of parts has reduced scrap costs. For some jobs, scrap has been reduced by 35 percent.

Because of the reduced part development costs and savings achieved by nesting, the company schedules its CNC machine to full capacity before allocating any production to tracing machines.

The use of CNC software has allowed the service center to be more aggressive in sales. The ability to produce and nest parts quickly at the quotation phase allows it to calculate accurate estimates of material utilization and production times.

The use of CNC software has resulted in reductions in part development time, scrap, plate handling, and production time. These factors have helped reduce lead times and increase the company's flexibility.

Case Study 2

Case Study 2 focuses on Merz Metal and Machine of Buffalo, New York. The company is a sheet metal fabricator specializing in ventilation, pollution control, and material handling systems.

The company had been using CNC profile cutting equipment and CNC software since 1981, when management recognized that the layout and cutting of sheet metal parts was the bottleneck in the manufacturing process.

So, the primary motivations for the investment in CNC were the automation of the sheet metal cutting process and elimination of manual layout of three-dimensional parts.

The use of a parametric program has allowed

the company to eliminate almost all of the layout work needed to produce fittings for ventilation and piping systems. Fittings that would have required hours of layout and development work by skilled personnel can now be produced in seconds.

The savings are even greater since the flat-plate layout is in the form of a CNC program, ready for use with the profile cutting machine.

The speed and accuracy of this part development software has allowed complex fittings like reducing elbows and asymmetric Y-joints to be used. Before, these types of fittings would have been too expensive to produce.

The company has realized several unexpected benefits from automating the part development and cutting process. The improved accuracy of the computerized layout process as well as cutting has reduced costs in other manufacturing areas like fit-up and welding.

Improved quality and greater design flexibility has also translated into higher customer satisfaction.

The company has realized additional savings by using nesting software. Currently, 80 percent of all sheet metal parts produced are nested.

Management estimates that nesting has reduced overall material use by 20 percent. Reduced material handling and improved cutting machine throughput are also benefits of nesting.

Because of the diverse nature of its product line, the company has spent as much on CNC software as it has on the profile cutting machine. Management feels that, with reasonable production volume, payback periods for this type of investment should be no longer than six months to one year.

Benefits

The following is a summary of some of the benefits of integrated use of CNC part development and nesting software with CNC profile cutting equipment:

1. Eliminates drafting of templates as well as the problems associated with template storage and handling.

2. Eliminates manual layout time, and part development does not require a skilled layout person.

3. Improves accuracy, resulting in better quality and reduced costs in other areas such as fit-up, welding, and finishing.

4. Minimizes redundant geometry definition by using CAD information. Also reduces chance for errors.

5. Additional capabilities encourage use of alternative design solutions.

6. Reduces scrap.

7. Reduces plate handling.

8. Improves profile cutting machine throughput.

Limitations

Like the implementation of any new technology, the use of CNC part development and nesting software presents problems as well as opportunities.

1. Experience and knowledge of the manufacturing processes are important attributes of a skilled fabricator. The effective use of CNC software does require some level of computer competency. Finding personnel with skills in both areas can be a challenge.

Identification of the ability and desire of a person to learn new technology is a key to the successful transfer from manual to computerized methods. It is also vital to recognize the role of training in the transition period.

2. The use of CNC part development and cutting will usually lead to dependence on this technology. Attention must be paid to ensure that important skills are not concentrated in a single person. As with any critical part of an operation, there should be some level of redundancy to protect against the unexpected.

3. A common problem in adopting parametric part development is that the software, however flexible, may use a different method to implement a given design. It is important to realize that it is not always wrong to use an approach that is different than the familiar one that has always been used.

Flexibility is a key factor in getting the most out of new technology. If using an existing approach is important, alternative or even custom software might have to be considered.

Impact on Other Areas

As CNC shape cutting technology is implemented, it is important to recognize that other areas of the business will be impacted.

Obviously, production planning will have to be aware of changes in manufacturing costs and capabilities in the development and production of profile cut parts. Attention should also be paid to other areas that will be affected, such as fit-up, welding, and finishing.

New production methods will also impact the process of cost estimating and sales. It will be important that everyone in the organization understand the effects of new manufacturing methods.

For management, the implementation of CNC profile cutting technology can present new opportunities. Automated nesting systems are well-suited to integration with JIT and Work-In-Process (WIP) manufacturing. CNC software can provide the opportunity to enter new markets or provide new services to existing customers.

Summary

CNC profile cutting technology has never been more affordable. With reasonable planning and attention to implementation details, the payback for the investment in this technology can be surprisingly quick.

Modern CNC profile cutting equipment provides the opportunity to make the manufacture of parts cut from sheet or plate material effective and efficient. CNC part development and nesting software are the key to making the most of that opportunity.

How to choose abrasive cutoff wheels for steel fabrication

In today's competitive marketplace, even routine manufacturing operations should be monitored to optimize productivity and cut costs. A case in point is cutoff operations.

In a typical fabricating operation, the simplest cutoff application may use hundreds of wheels a year. If a user chooses the wrong wheel, a significant amount of money could be wasted.

All too often, cutoff wheels are purchased on price alone, when, in fact, the most important determinants of grinding efficiency are rate of cut and wheel life. The key to success is selecting the right wheel for the particular cutoff job.

The Fundamentals

Abrasive cutoff wheels are considered the fastest method for cutting a range of metals and nonmetallic materials to precise dimensions. Unlike a conventional grinding wheel that abrades away the surface of the workpiece, cutoff wheels are designed to cut through the workpiece.

In cutting off, a wheel may produce a burr or burning discoloration. This may or may not be tolerable, depending on the job requirements. In sheet metal fabrication, the objective usually is to produce cuts with little or no burr or burn.

When the various components of a cutoff wheel and the way they interact is understood, the best wheel can be chosen for a particular job.

Wheel Markings: What They Mean

An example of a wheel marking for a typical cutoff wheel — 4 inches by .035 inch by ¼ inch — used for cutting stainless steel sheet is this:

A 60 - O B NA2/Sides D

Abrasives and Grit Size. Cutoff wheels are usually made with one of two abrasives: aluminum oxide, the "A" in the example, for metals, and silicon carbide, designated as "C" in wheel markings, for nonmetals.

Grit sizes range from coarse (24) for faster stick removal and longer life to fine (120) for minimized burring, as on thin-wall tubing. The 60 grit in the example will give both reasonable life and little or no burr.

Grade. Grade refers to the hardness of the wheel or, looked at another way, the strength of the bonding material.

Cutoff wheels range in grade from hard (X,Y,Z) for greater wheel durability to soft (H,J) for better cutting quality, particularly on hard-to-cut materials. The "O" grade in the example falls near the middle of the range.

In general, coarse, hard wheels have long life but produce a burr on the cut end of the workpiece. Fine, soft wheels offer shorter product life but produce little or no burring.

Bond. Cutoff wheel bonds are available to

meet the full range of requirements from high-volume production to the highest quality cuts. They fall into three types:

1. Resin, indicated by the "B" in the example, for dry (and sometimes wet) cutting

2. Rubber, indicated by an "R," usually for wet applications

3. Shellac, indicated by an "E," for top-quality wet or dry cutting, such as salvaging broken high-speed steel drills in the toolroom

Reinforcement. To add strength and stability to the wheel in severe cross-bending applications, manufacturers sometimes mold a fiberglass material into the wheel.

Reinforced wheels are required when the wheel is hand-guided or the workpiece is not securely clamped. The "NA2" portion of the sample specification indicates full external reinforcement.

Side Patterns. Cutoff wheels are made with different side patterns to meet special cutoff situations. Side patterns provide relief (i.e., counterset) in the cut. They vary in form by manufacturer, bond type, and severity of the job. "Sides D" is most common on smaller wheels.

Horsepower "Rule of Thumb"

When purchasing or rebuilding an abrasive cutoff machine, the recommendations of the manufacturer should be followed. However, the horsepower (HP) "rule of thumb" should also be kept in mind: a cutoff machine should have at least 1 HP per inch of wheel diameter.

If HP is less than the wheel diameter, a softer grade (N,P) wheel may have to be used to avoid stalling motors, glazed wheels, and burned parts.

If HP is greater than the wheel diameter, a harder grade (V,X,Z) can probably be used, which costs no more and gives better wheel life.

Optimizing Cost Savings

To minimize costs and maximize the productivity of any abrasive cutoff operation, follow these guidelines:

1. To improve wheel life, use the coarsest grit and hardest grade that will produce an acceptable part.

2. Make cuts as fast as possible; use all available HP.

3. Run the wheel as close to maximum speed as possible, but do not exceed it.

4. Use a feed rate as fast as possible commensurate with available HP.

5. Orient the workpiece securely.

6. Keep the machine in top form. Worn spindle bearings and inadequate clamping devices can affect cutoff wheel efficiency and generate unnecessary wheel breakage.

Additionally, keep abreast of improvements in abrasives. The materials and technology used to make cutoff wheels are constantly changing.

If the same cutoff wheels have been used for more than five years, they are probably obsolete.

Finally, and most importantly, total cutoff costs must be analyzed and evaluated.

Authors' Index

- -

Chapter One: Sawing

"Selecting a metal cutting saw: How to avoid buying the wrong machine," p. 1
(from *The FABRICATOR®*, May 1992)

John Stong
Saw Sales and Technical Support Manager
Dake
724 Robbins Road
Grand Haven, Michigan 49417-2603
Phone: 616-842-7110
Fax: 616-842-0859

"Factors affecting band saw cutting performance: Making your sawing operation a profit-making function," p. 5 (from *The FABRICATOR*, May 1993)

H E & M, Inc.
P.O. Box 1148
Pryor, Oklahoma 74362-1148
Phone: 918-825-1000
Fax: 918-825-7279

"Precision sawing adds value for end users: How to precision cut plate and extrusions for a profit," p. 14 (from *The FABRICATOR*, October 1989)

Kenneth E. Forman
President
Metl-Saw Systems, Inc.
2950-A Bay Vista Court
Benicia, California 94510
Phone: 707-746-6200
Fax: 707-746-5085

Chapter Two: Lasers

"Selecting and justifying a laser cutting system: Examining the benefits of lasers," p. 19 (from *The FABRICATOR*, October 1992)

Michael Pellecchia
Former Assistant Manager
U.S. Amada Ltd.
Laser Division
7025 Firestone Boulevard
Buena Park, California 90621-1869
Phone: 714-739-2111
Fax: 714-670-1439

"Justifying CO_2 laser cutting: Reviewing machine configurations and machine purchasing criteria," p. 29 (from *The FABRICATOR*, July/August 1990)

Bill Kramp
Former Sales Manager
TRUMPF Inc.
Farmington Industrial Park
Farmington, Connecticut 06032
Phone: 203-677-9741
Fax: 203-678-1704

"Five-axis CO_2 laser machine tools and laser machining," p. 32   (from "Lasers in Fabricating" conference, April 1990)

Dale Davis
Department Manager
U.S. Amada Ltd.
Research and Development Department
7025 Firestone Boulevard
Buena Park, California 90621-1869
Phone: 714-739-2111
Fax: 714-739-4099

"Replacing other fabricating operations with laser cutting: Applications ranging from stamping to tube cutting," p. 43 (from *The FABRICATOR*, September 1991)

Terry VanderWert
Director of Marketing
Lumonics Corporation
Eden Prairie Operations
6690 Shady Oak Road
Eden Prairie, Minnesota 55344-3200
Phone: 612-941-9530
Fax: 612-941-7611

"Why isn't there a laser in every sheet metal job shop?: Why European and Japanese shops buy more laser cutters than the U.S.," p. 45   (from *The FABRICATOR*, October 1990)

Leonard Migliore
Former Applications Manager
U.S. Amada Ltd.
Laser Division
7025 Firestone Boulevard
Buena Park, California 90621-1869
Phone: 714-739-2111
Fax: 714-670-1439

Donald Hoffman
Former Division Manager
U.S. Amada Ltd.
Laser Division
7025 Firestone Boulevard
Buena Park, California 90621-1869
Phone: 714-739-2111
Fax: 714-670-1439

"Laser cutting special materials and shapes: Defining unsuitable areas for laser processing," p. 47 (from T*he FABRICATOR*, May/June 1989)

Mazak Nissho Iwai Corporation
140 East State Parkway
Schaumburg, Illinois 60173-5335
Phone: 708-882-8777
Fax: 708-882-0191

"Staying competitive using five-axis laser clean cutting: How to improve the quality of three-dimensional parts," p. 52 (from *The FABRICATOR*, September 1990)

Laser Industries, Inc.
677 North Hariton Street
Orange, California 92668
Phone: 714-532-3271
Fax: 714-639-6941
Contact: John Butterly

"Control of variables crucial to laser performance: A discussion of the factors affecting laser cut quality," p. 57 (from *The FABRICATOR*, January/February 1989)

> Howard S. Abbott (deceased)
> C. Behrens Machinery Company
> Danvers Industrial Park
> Danvers, Massachusetts 01923
> Phone: 508-774-4200
> Fax: 508-774-0532

"Reducing heat effect: How to lessen thermal damage in laser cut parts," p. 60 (from *The FABRICATOR*, October 1989)

> Strippit, Inc.
> A Unit of IDEX
> 12975 Clarence Center Road
> Akron, New York 14001-1321
> Phone: 716-542-4511
> Fax: 716-542-5957

"Improving laser cutting quality in humid weather: How to beat cooled optics condensation," p. 62 (from *The FABRICATOR*, July/August 1991)

> E.W. Rapp
> President
> Rapp Machinery
> 3914 Wesley
> P.O. Box 8305
> Greenville, Texas 75404-8305
> Phone: 903-455-2311
> Fax: 903-455-2317

"New developments in laser fusion cutting," p. 65 (from 1989 FABTECH International conference, ©1989 FABTECH, Fabricators & Manufacturers Association, International, and Society of Manufacturing Engineers)

> Daniel D. Dechamps
> President
> TRUMPF Inc.
> Farmington Industrial Park
> Farmington, Connecticut 06032
> Phone: 203-677-9741
> Fax: 203-678-1704

Chapter Three: Thermal Cutting

"Cutting with precision plasma technology: Stabilized jet helps improve cut quality,"
p. 71 (from *The FABRICATOR*, May 1993)

> James White
> Executive Vice President
> Komatsu Cutting Technologies, Inc.
> 200 Boston Avenue
> Medford, Massachusetts 02155-4243
> Phone: 617-396-1869
> Fax: 617-396-2280

"How to evaluate CNCs for thermal cutting: Design features and comparisons,"
p. 79 (from *The FABRICATOR*, April 1990)

> George Stelmaschuk
> Domestic Sales Manager
> Cleveland Machine Controls, Burny Division
> 7750 Hub Parkway
> Cleveland, Ohio 44125-5794
> Phone: 216-524-8800
> Fax: 216-642-2199

"Cost estimating and economics of thermal cutting: A down-to-earth look at plasma arc
and oxyfuel cutting costs," p. 83 (from T*he FABRICATOR*, January/February 1991.
Reprinted by permission of the American Welding Society)

> Jerry Karow
> Product Manager
> MG Industries
> W141 N9427 Fountain Boulevard
> Menomonee Falls, Wisconsin 53051
> Phone: 414-255-5520
> Fax: 414-255-5170

"Cutting steel for quality and safety," p. 90 (from *The FABRICATOR*, April 1990)

> Thomas Joos
> Marketing Director
> Broco, Inc.
> 2824 North Locust Avenue
> Rialto, California 92376-1749
> Phone: 714-350-4701
> Fax: 714-356-1426

"Retrofitting older flame cutting machinery: An alternative to purchasing new equipment,"
p. 93 (from *The FABRICATOR*, October 1992)

> Joseph Zak
> Cutting Machine Specialist and Independent Dealer for the
>   Burny Division of Cleveland Machine Controls
> Zak and Associates
> 196 Silver Lane
> Sunderland, Massachusetts 01375
> Phone: 413-665-3114
> Fax: 413-665-3114

Chapter Four: WATERJET

Waterjet cutting systems: Using high pressure for clean cutting," p. 99 (from *The FABRICATOR*,
April 1990)

> Ingersoll-Rand Waterjet Cutting Division
> 23629 Industrial Park Drive
> Farmington Hills, Michigan 48335-2857
> Phone: 313-471-0888
> Fax: 313-471-9113
> Contact: Rodie Woodard

"Procedure optimization and hardware improvements in abrasive waterjet cutting systems,"
p. 104 (from "Sheet Metal Applications: Bending, Folding, and Cutting" conference, July 1993)

> Kathy Zaring, Engineering Manager, Standard Products
> Glenn Erichsen, Research Engineer
> Charles Burnham, Director of Engineering
> Flow International Corporation
> 23500 64th Avenue South
> Kent, Washington 98032
> Phone: 206-850-3500
> Fax: 206-813-3285

"Fundamentals of waterjet technology: A discussion of high-pressure waterjet equipment selection for cutting and surface cleaning applications," p. 110 (from *The FABRICATOR*, April 1989)

Jay K. Guha
President
Monaken Technologies, Inc.
P.O. Box 13088
Pittsburgh, Pennsylvania 15243-0088
Phone: 412-221-1090
Fax: 412-221-1090

"Waterjet and laser methods offer alternatives for different applications: Factors to consider when choosing a cutting method," p. 114 (from *The FABRICATOR*, October 1990)

Charles Burnham
Director of Engineering
Flow International Corporation
23500 64th Avenue South
Kent, Washington 98032
Phone: 206-850-3500
Fax: 206-813-3285

Chapter Five: Other Technologies

"Profile cutting with CNC software: Gaining productivity through computer technology," p. 119   (from *The FABRICATOR*, May 1992)

John Rosenberg
CEO
Microcomputer Technology Consultants (MTC) Ltd.
P.O. Box 467
Lockport, New York 14095-0467
Phone: 716-433-7722
Fax: 716-433-1554

"How to choose abrasive cutoff wheels for steel fabrication," p. 125 (from *The FABRICATOR*, September 1990)

Peter Johnson
Senior Product Engineer
Norton Company
1 New Bond Street
Worcester, Massachusetts 01606-2614
Phone: 508-795-5599
Fax: 508-795-2187

Index

- -